WHIMSICAL COLORING BOOK FOR ADULTS

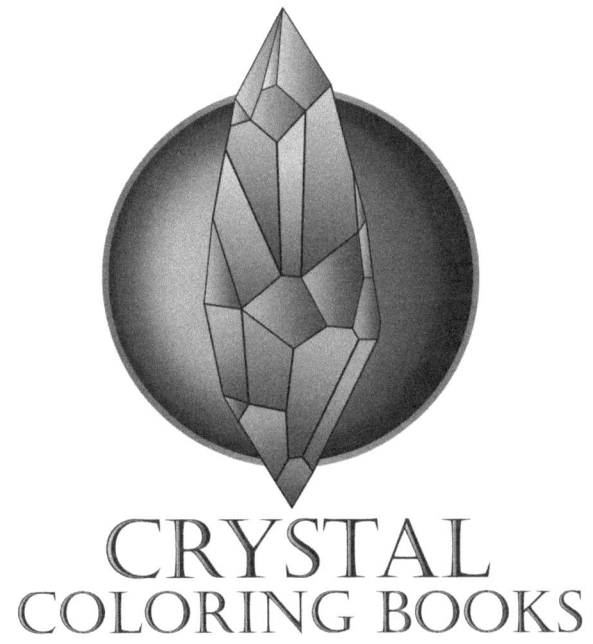

CRYSTAL COLORING BOOKS

Copyright © 2017 Crystal Coloring Books
All rights reserved.

ISBN: 9781790584840

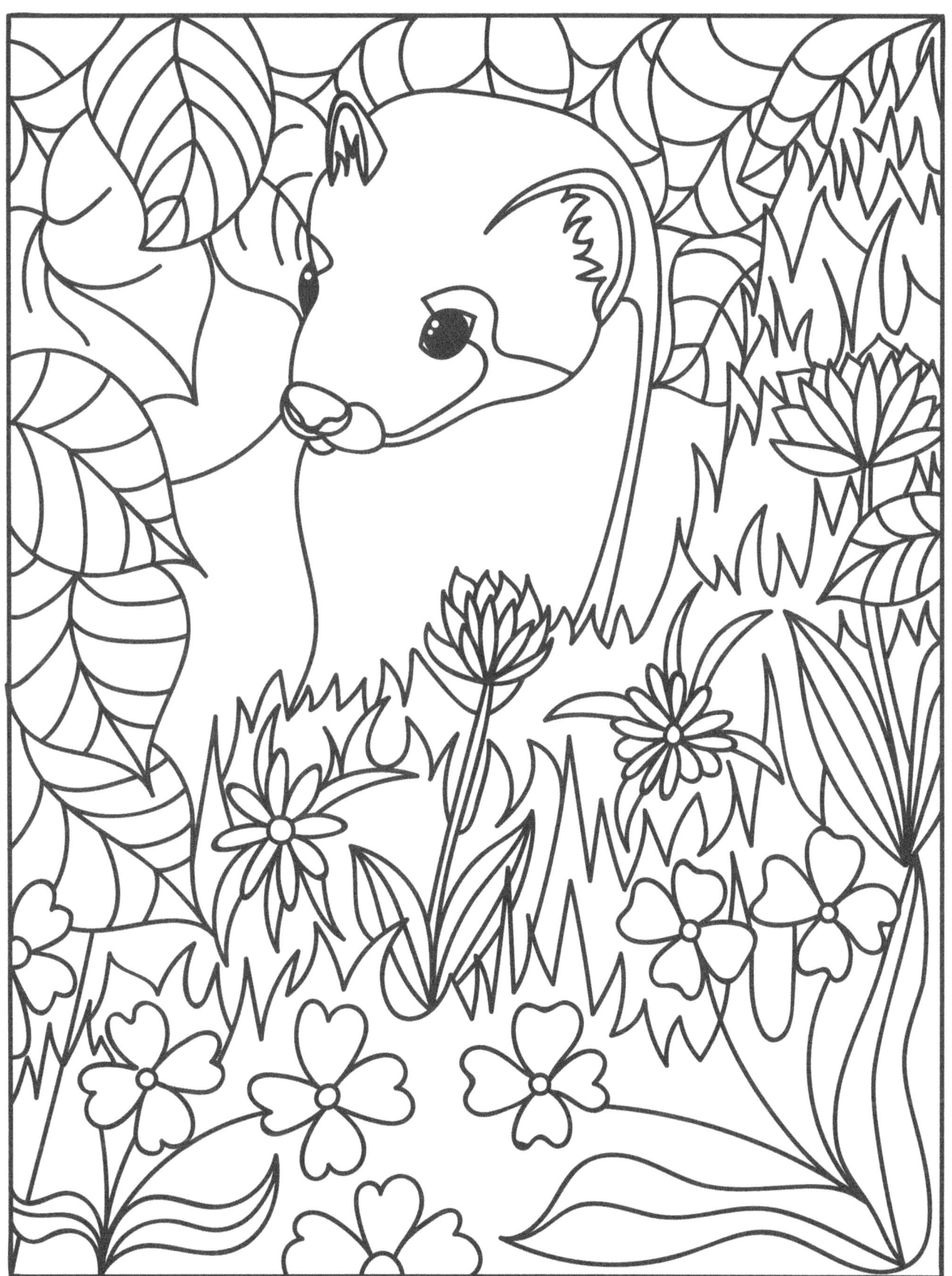

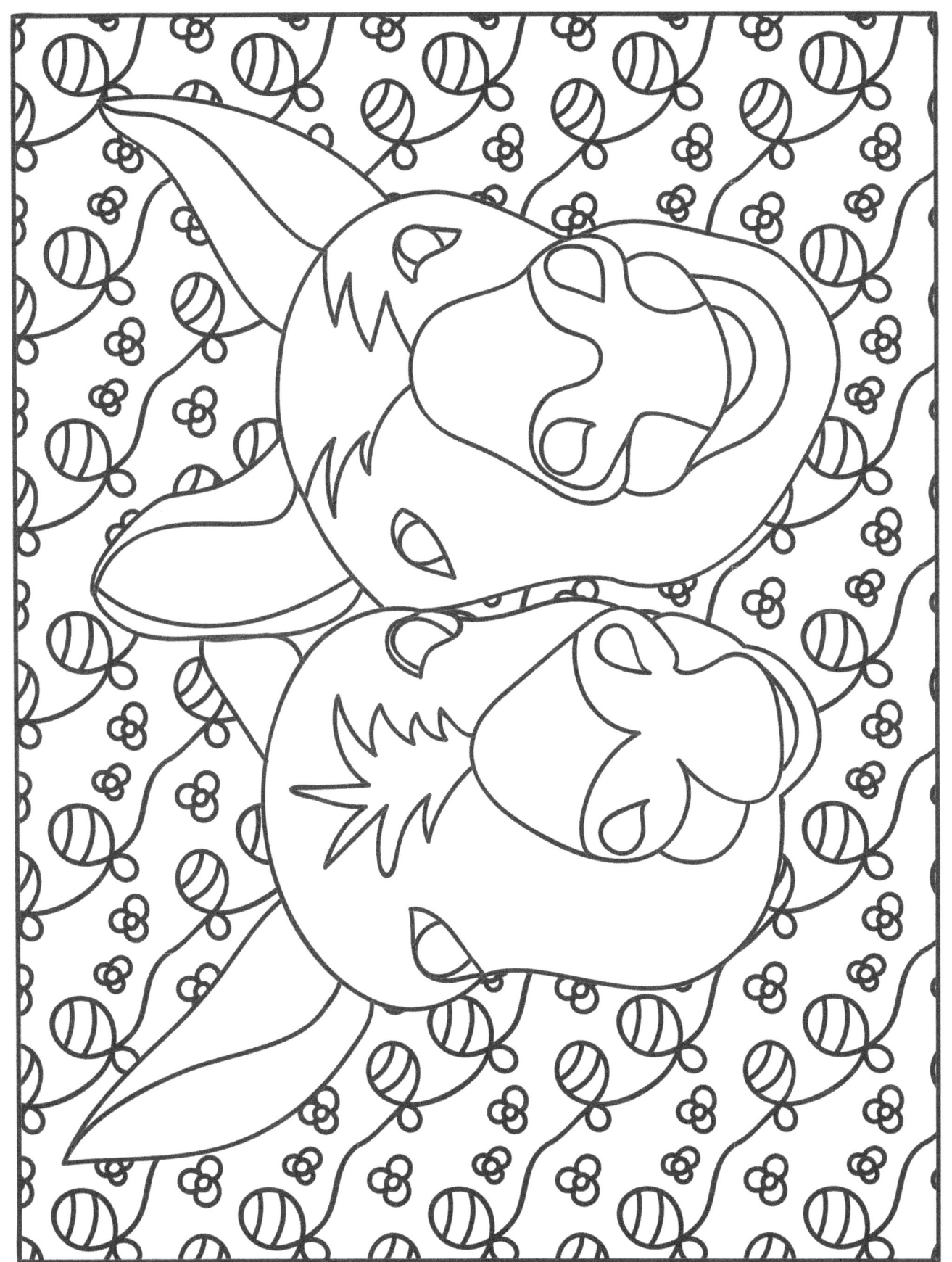

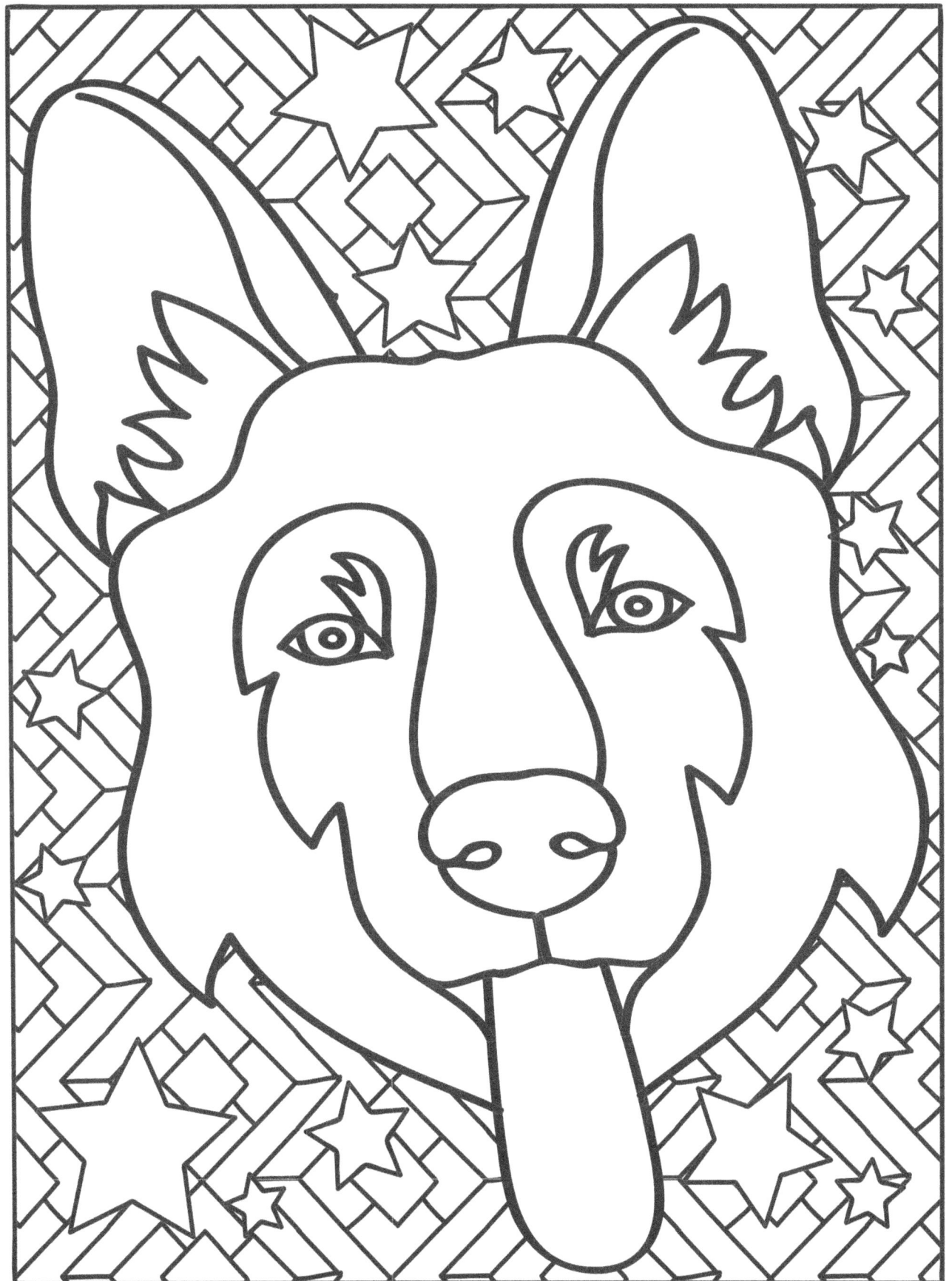

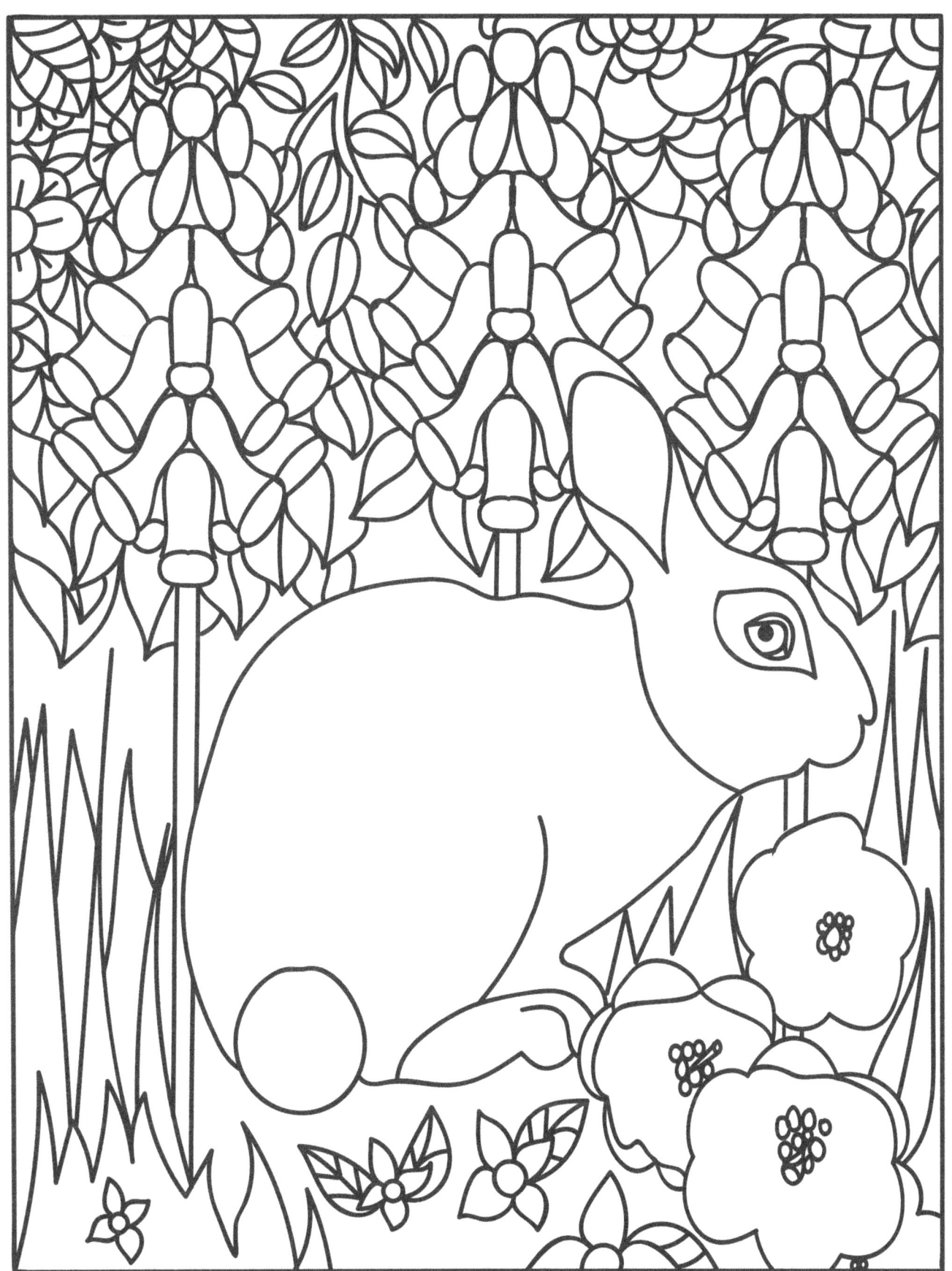

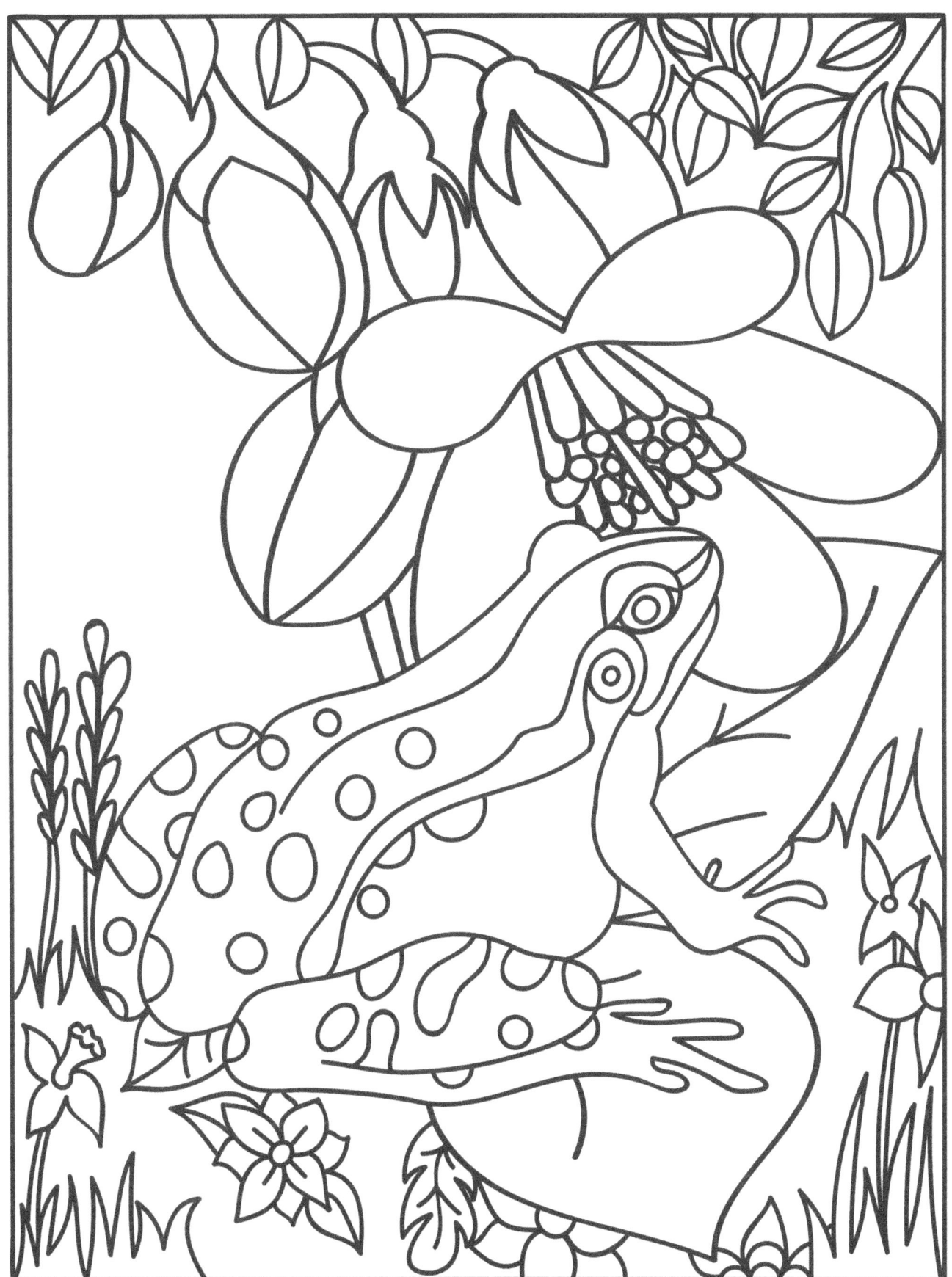

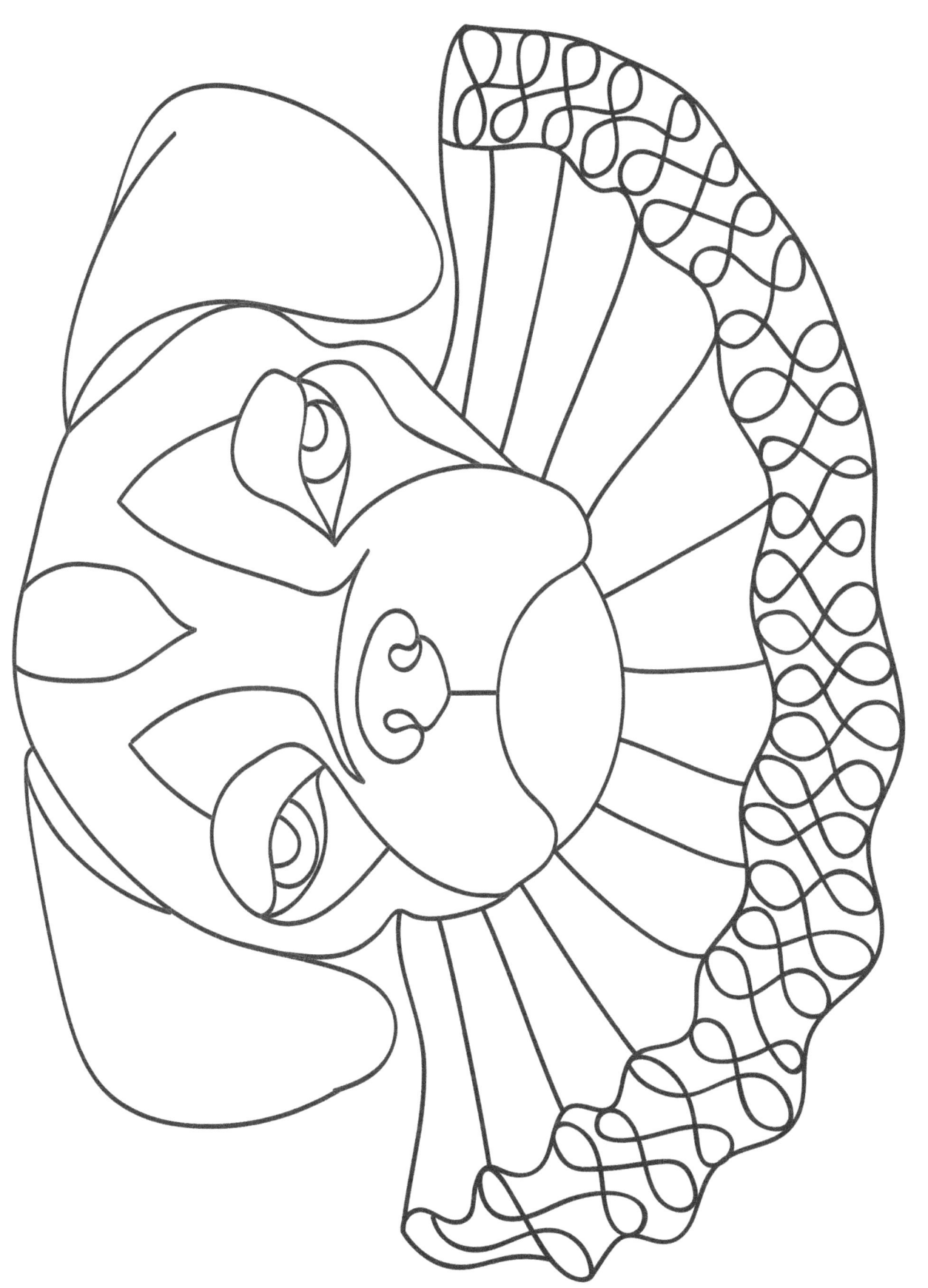

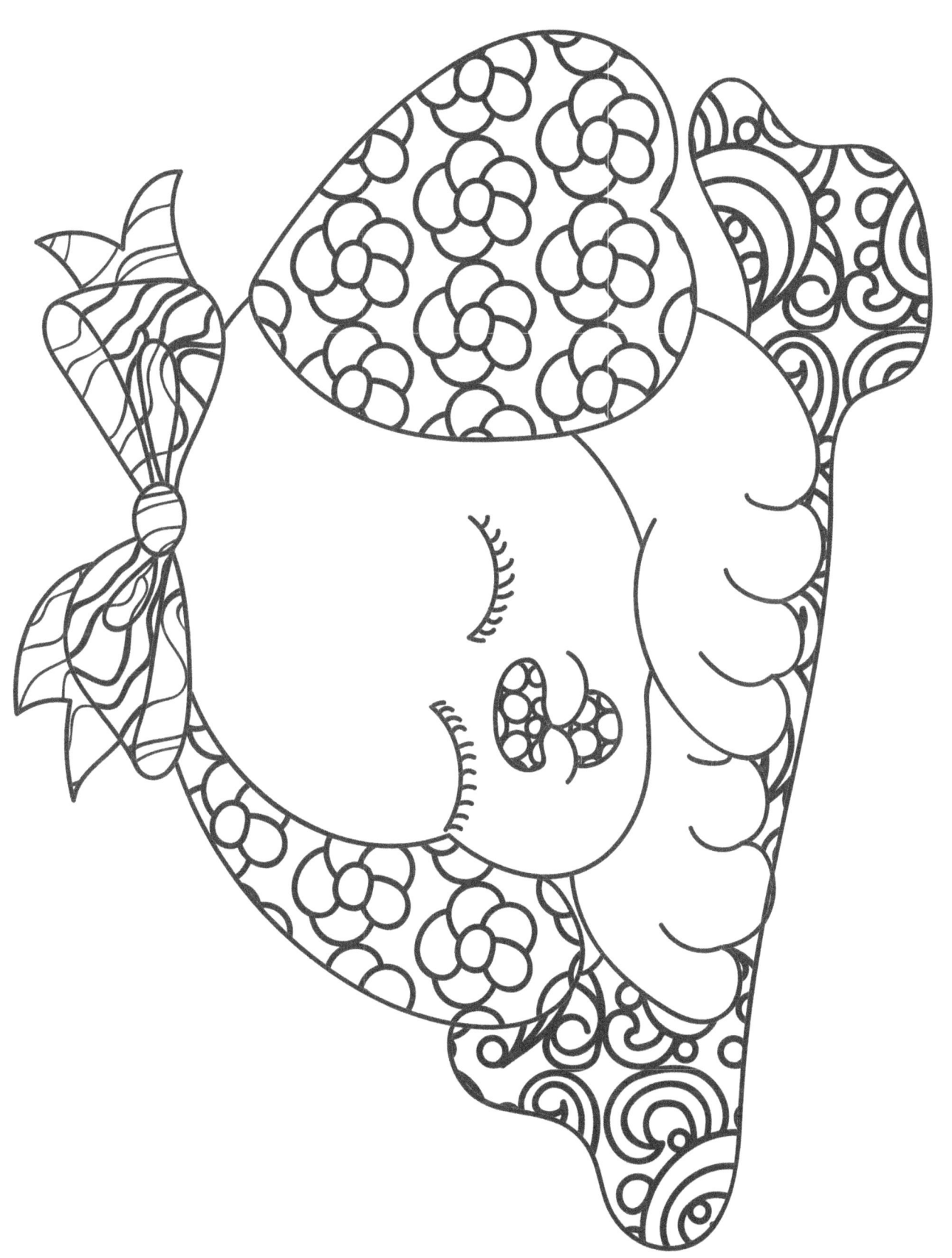

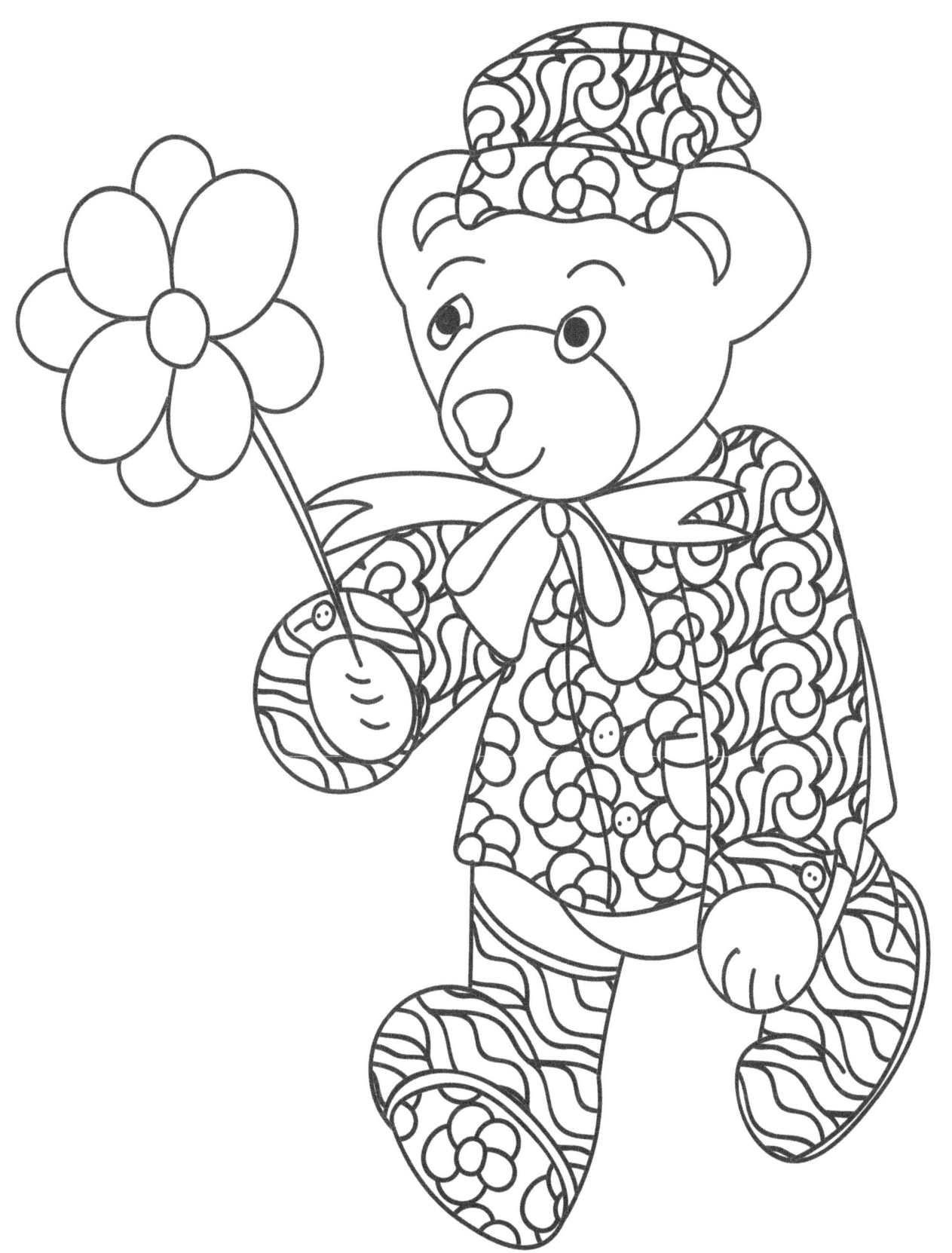

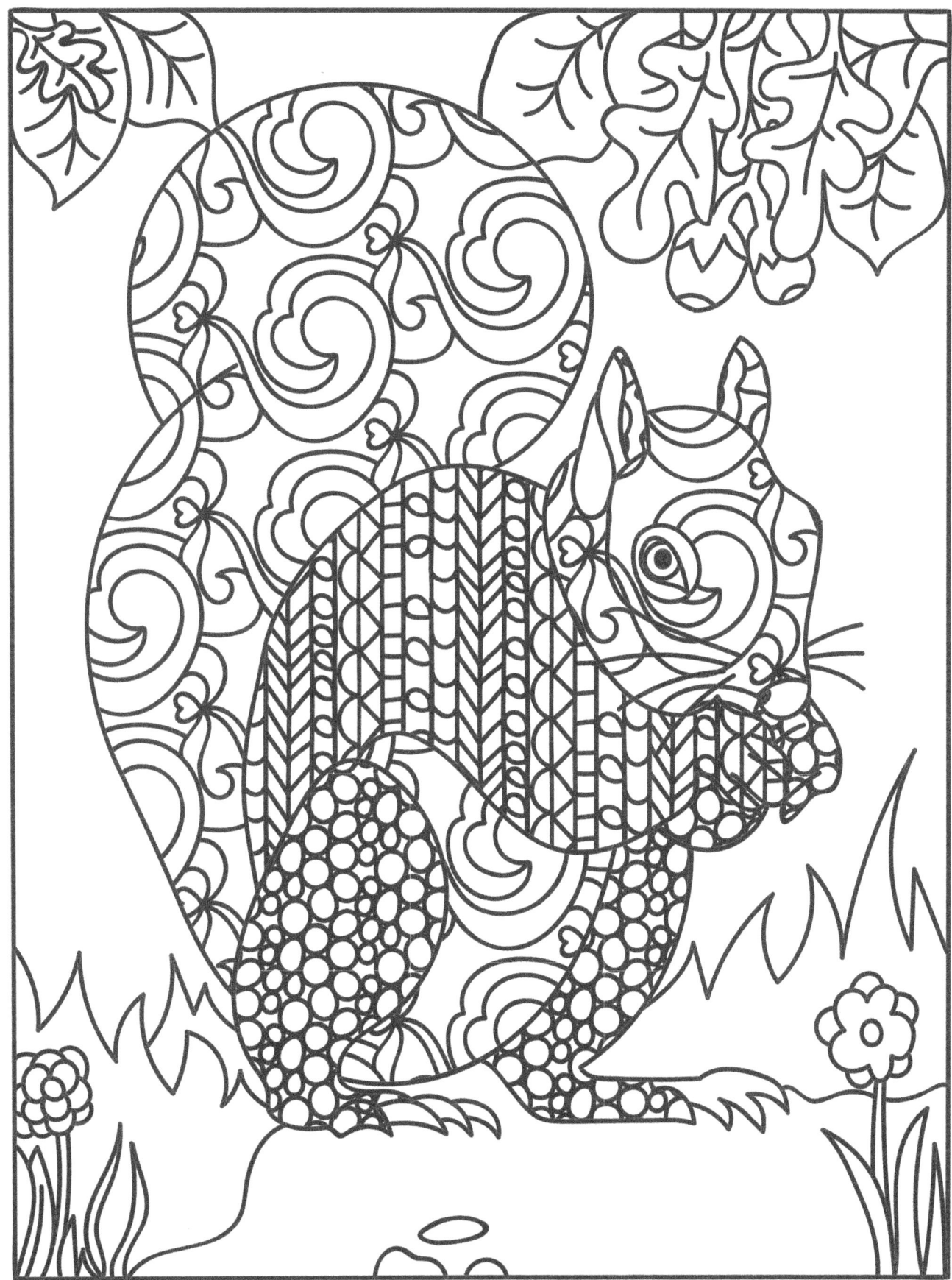

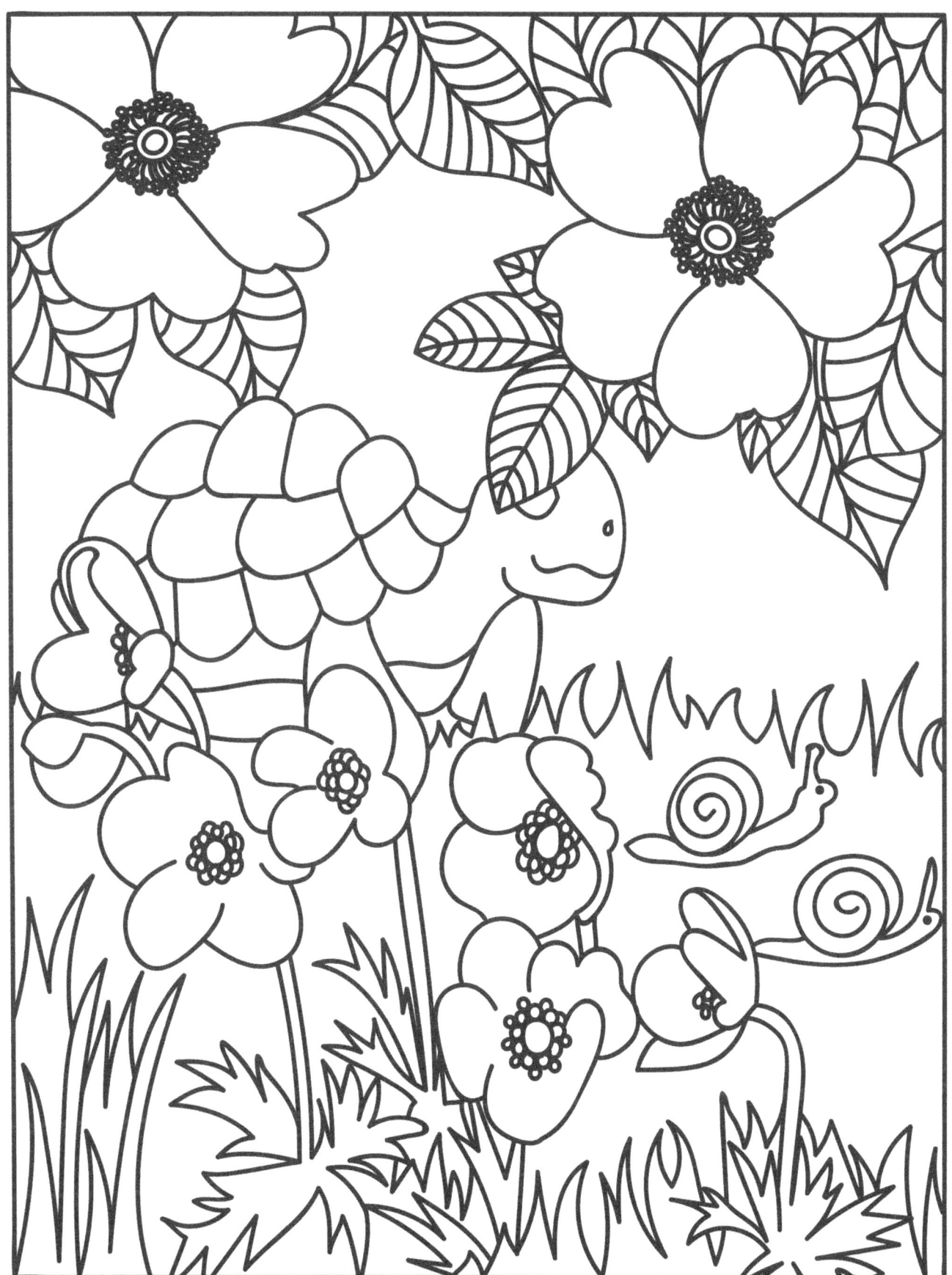

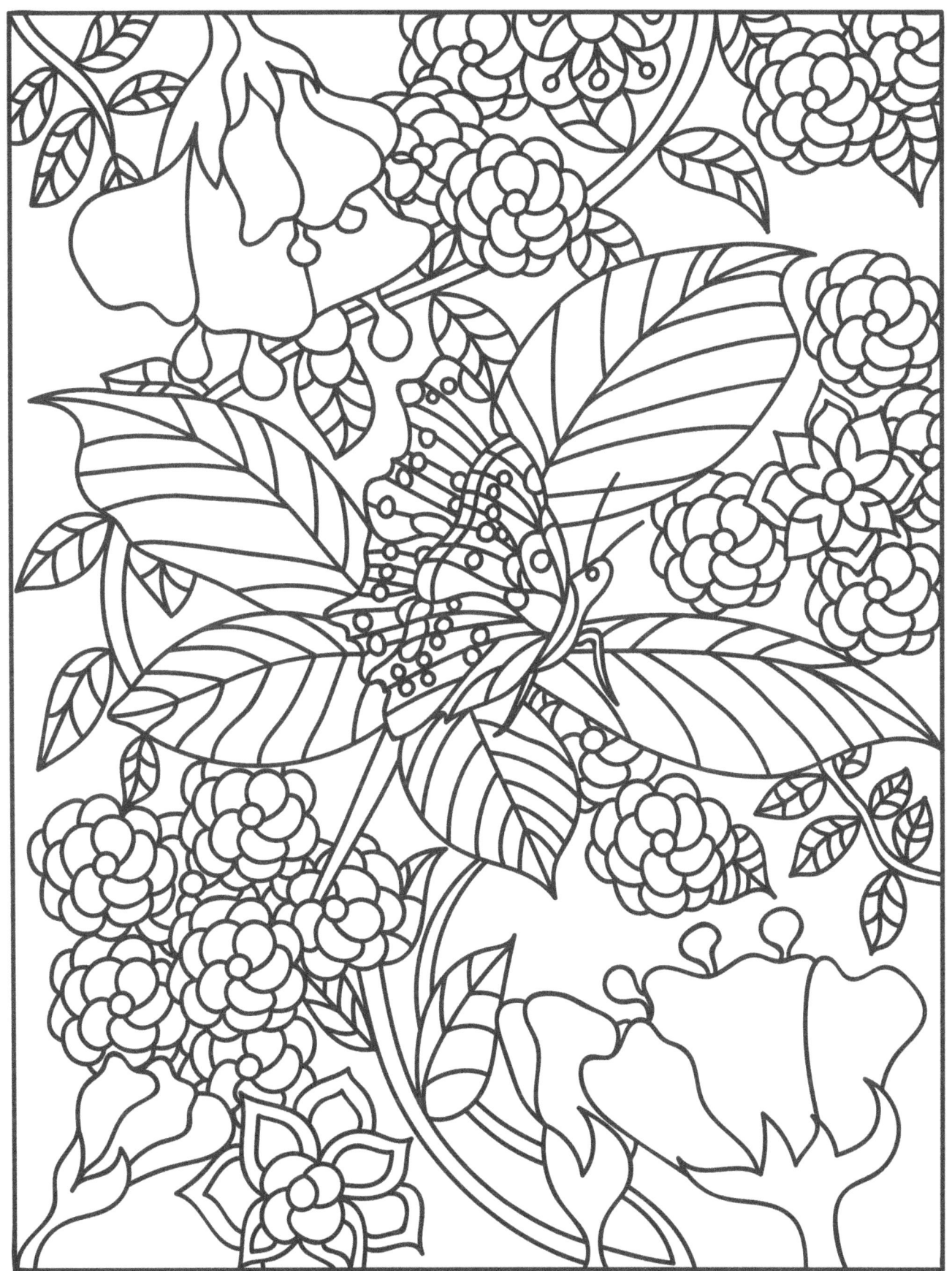

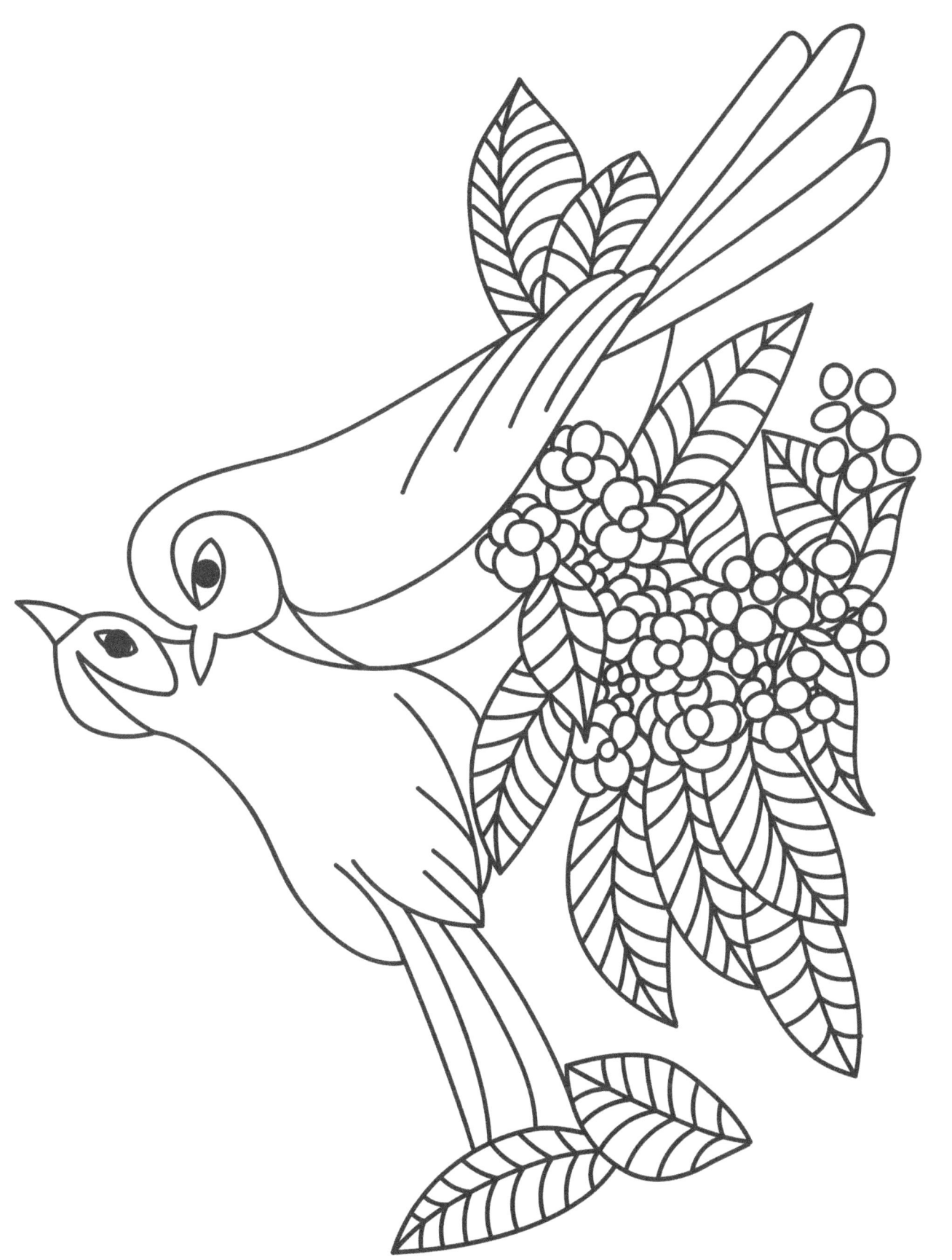

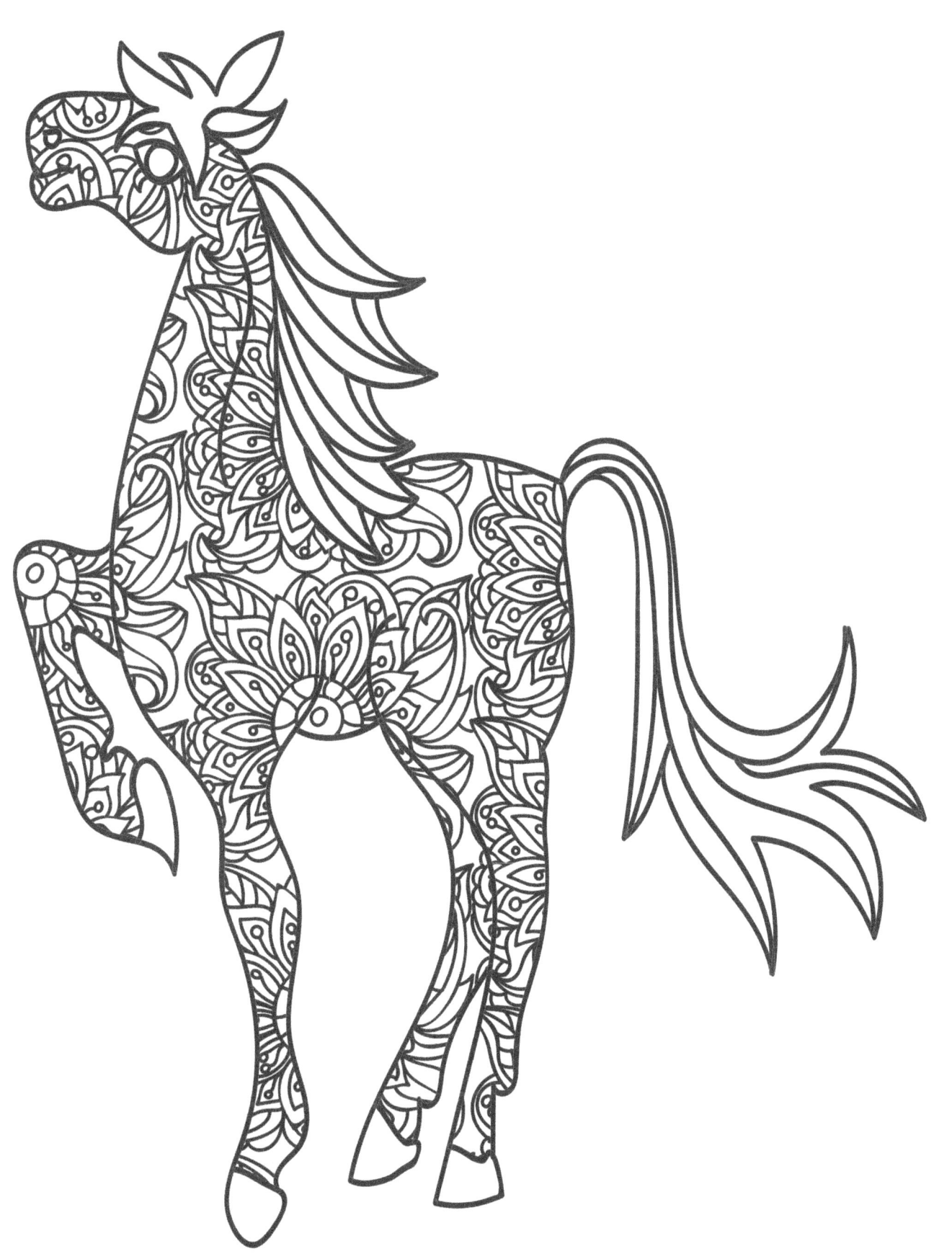

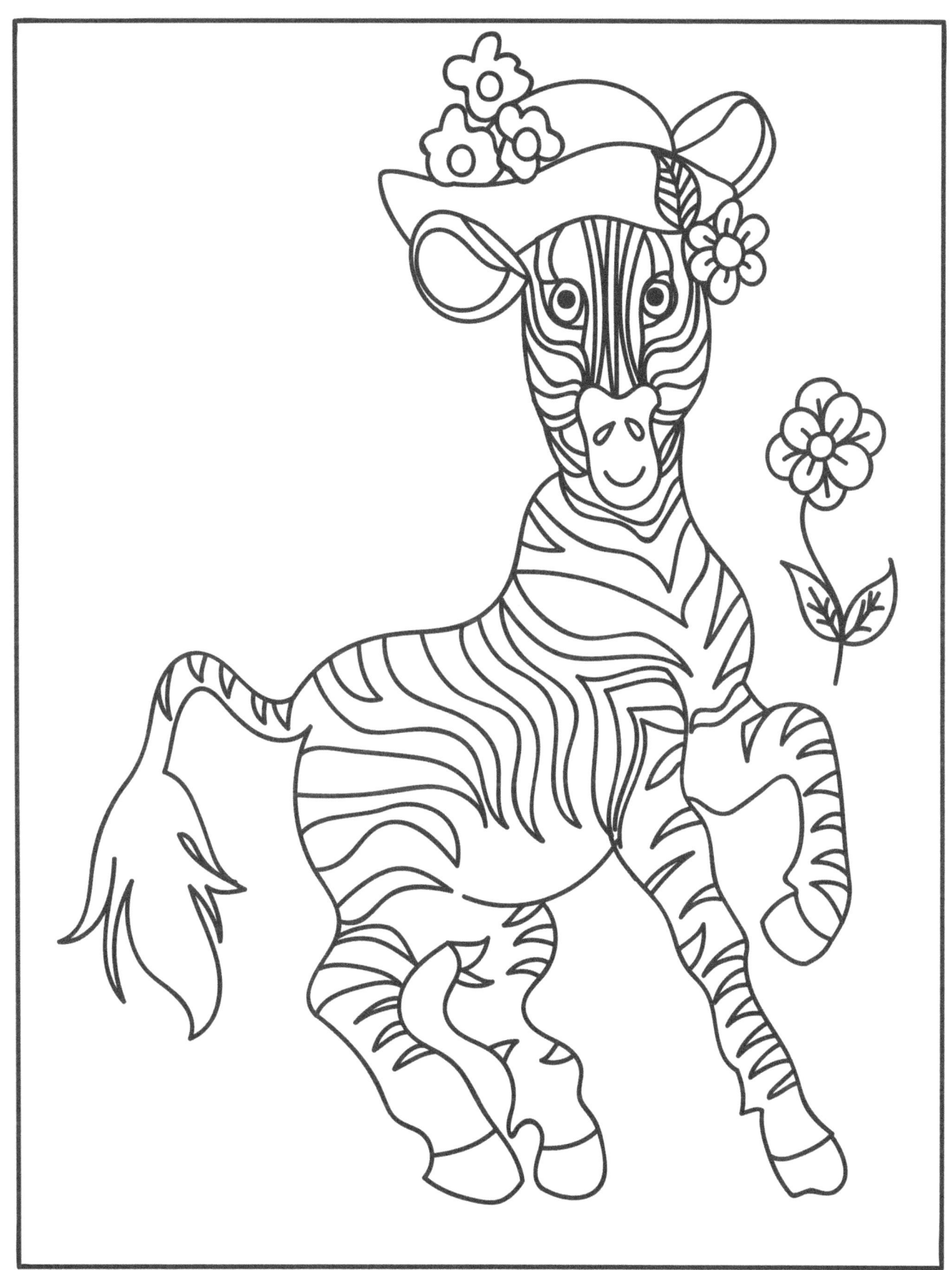

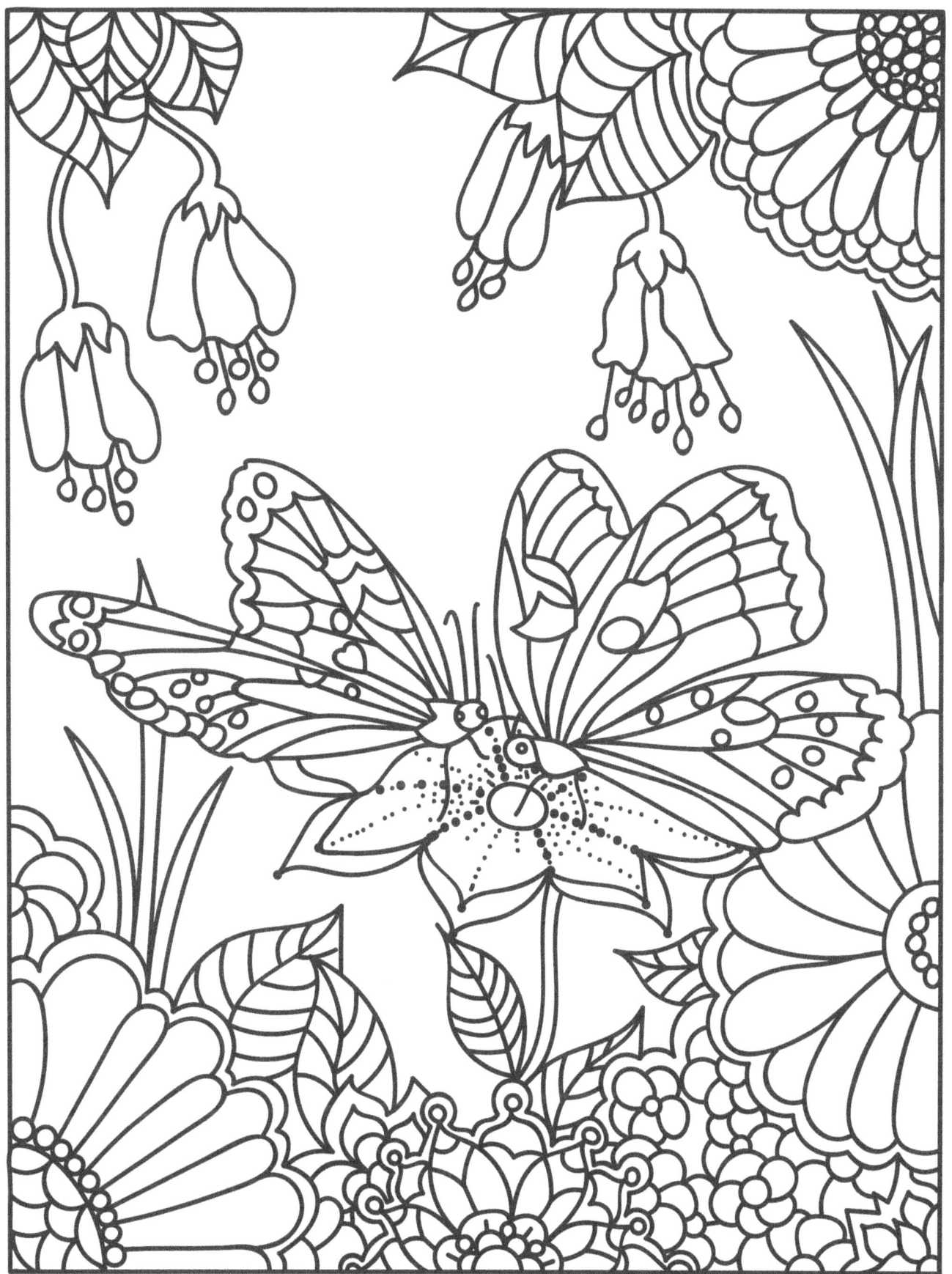

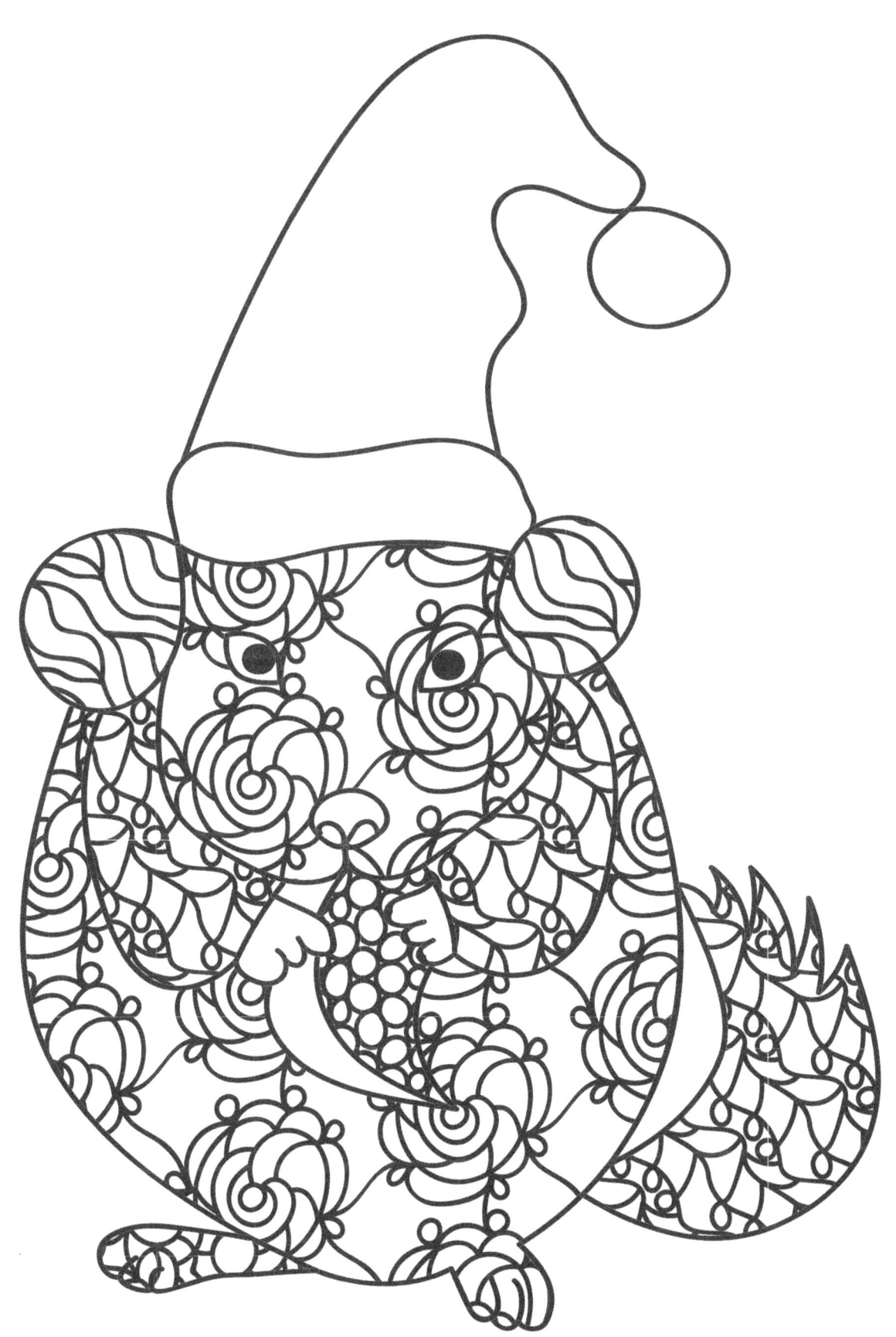

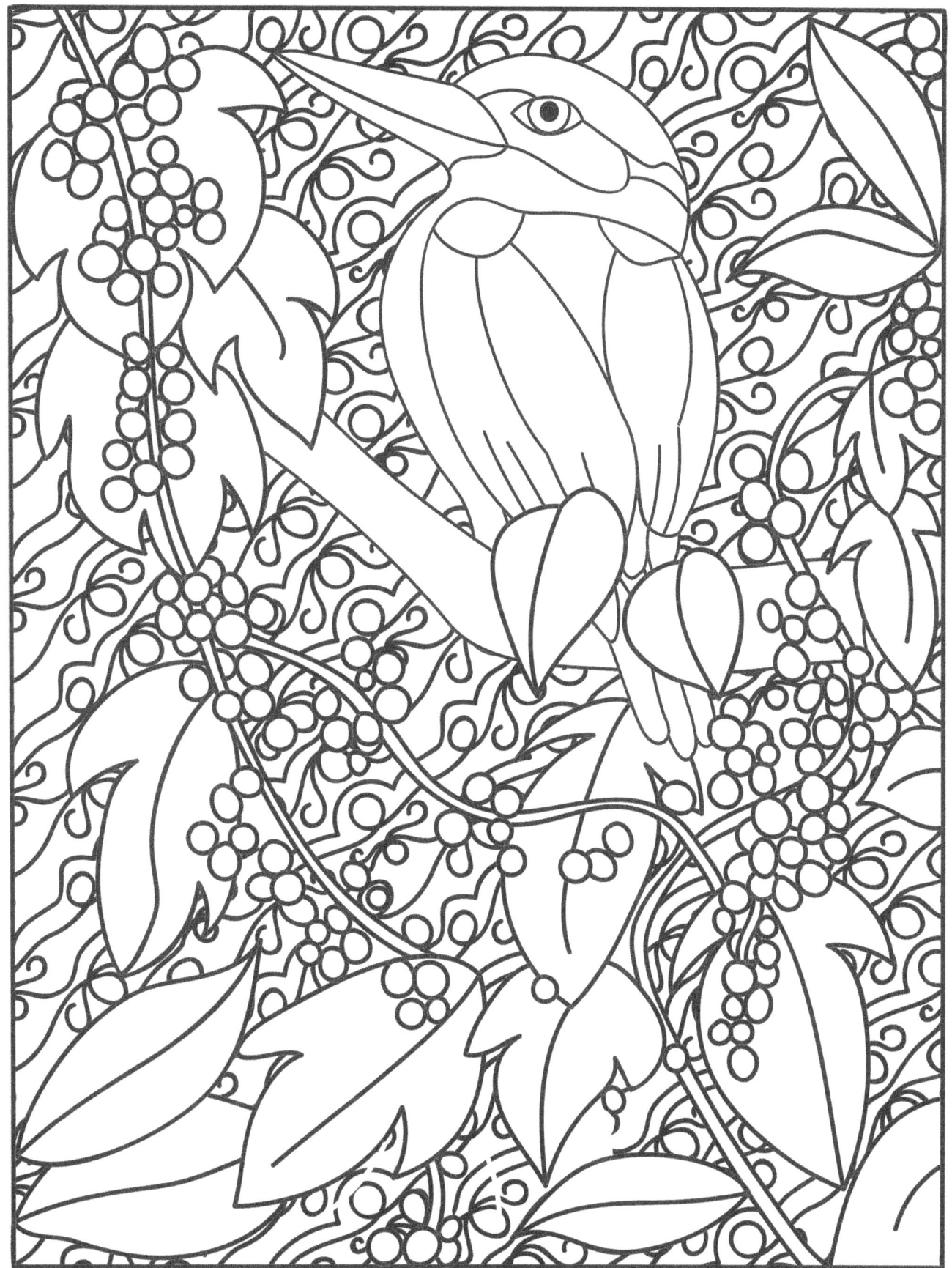

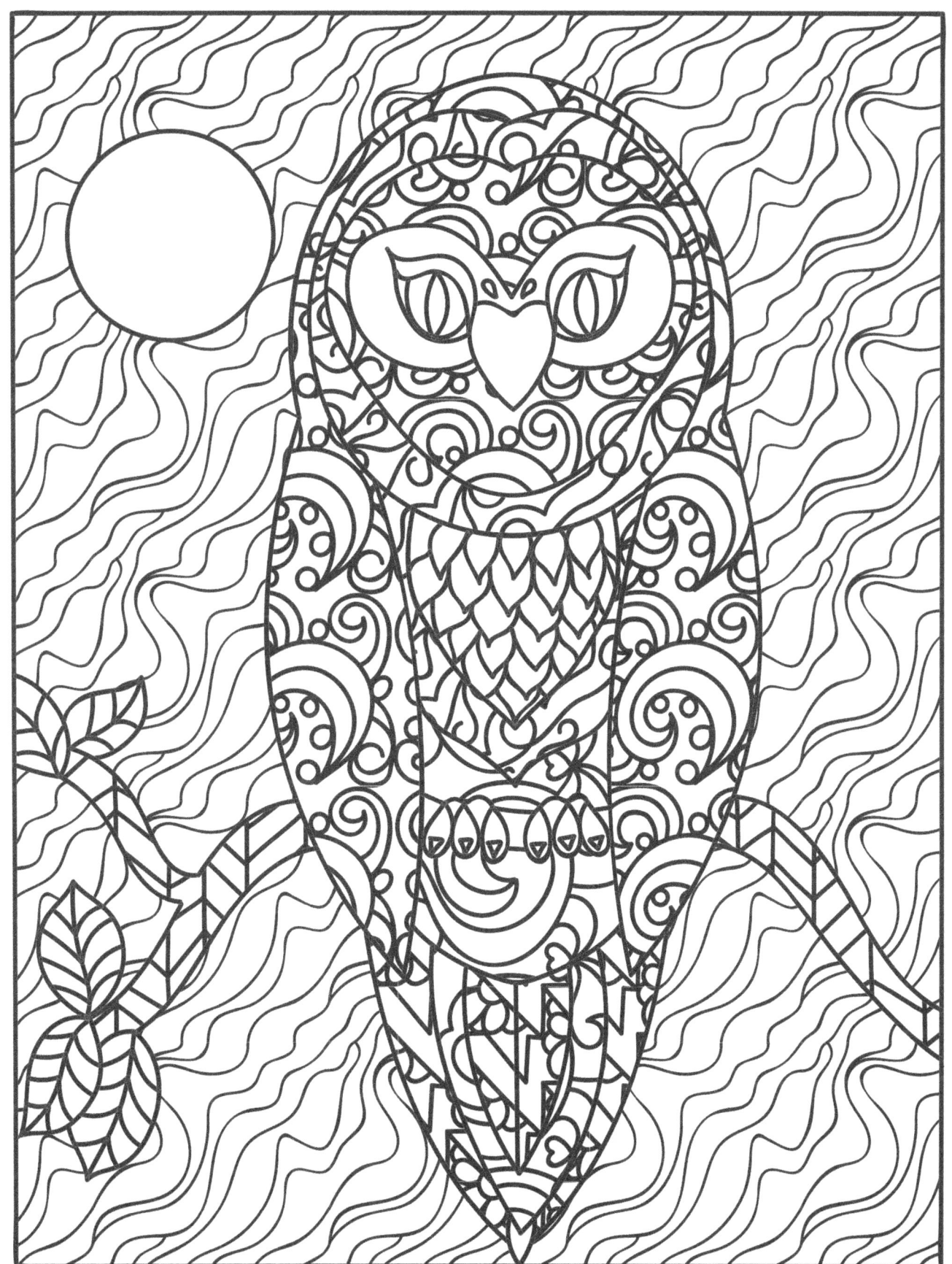

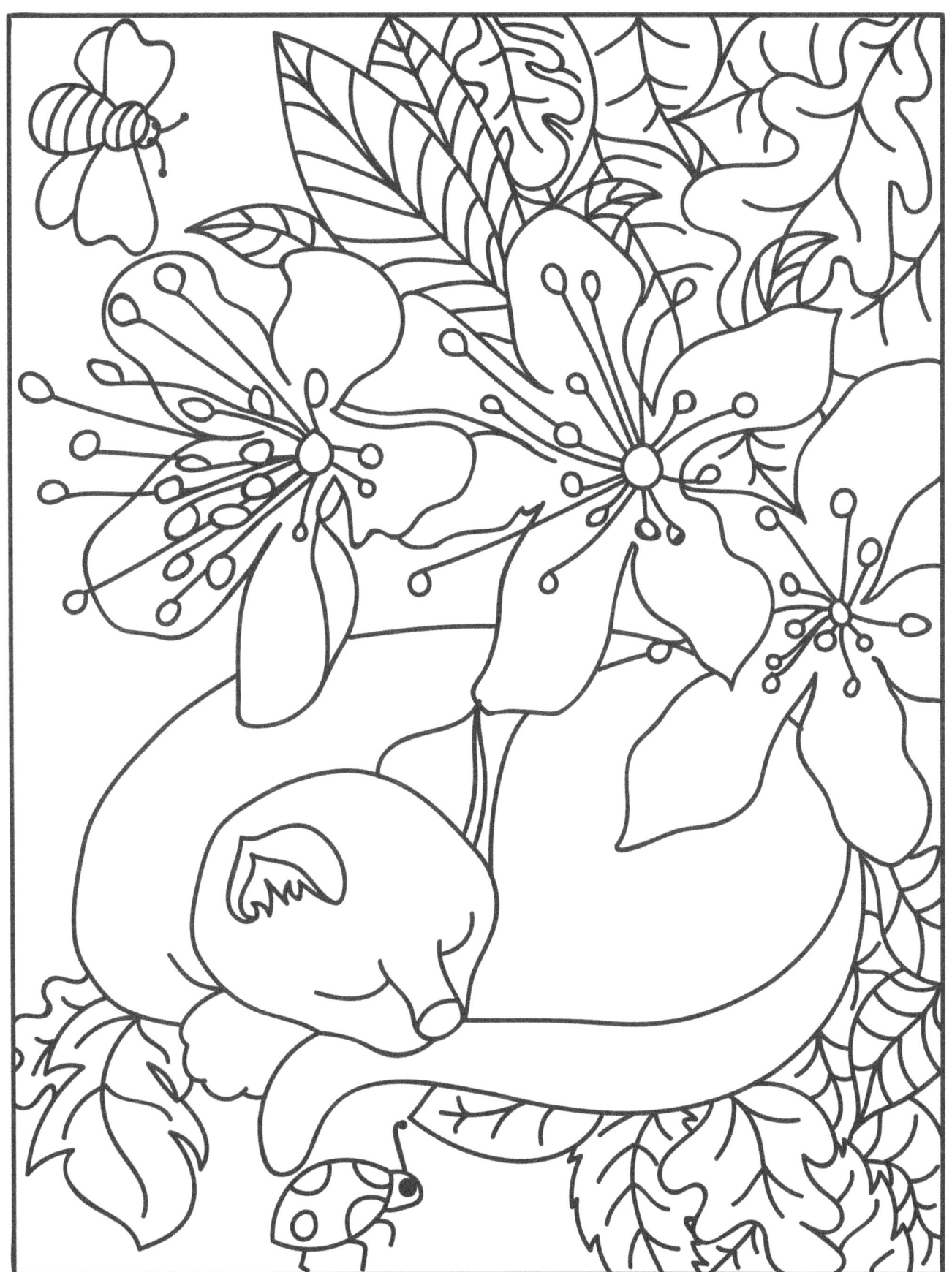

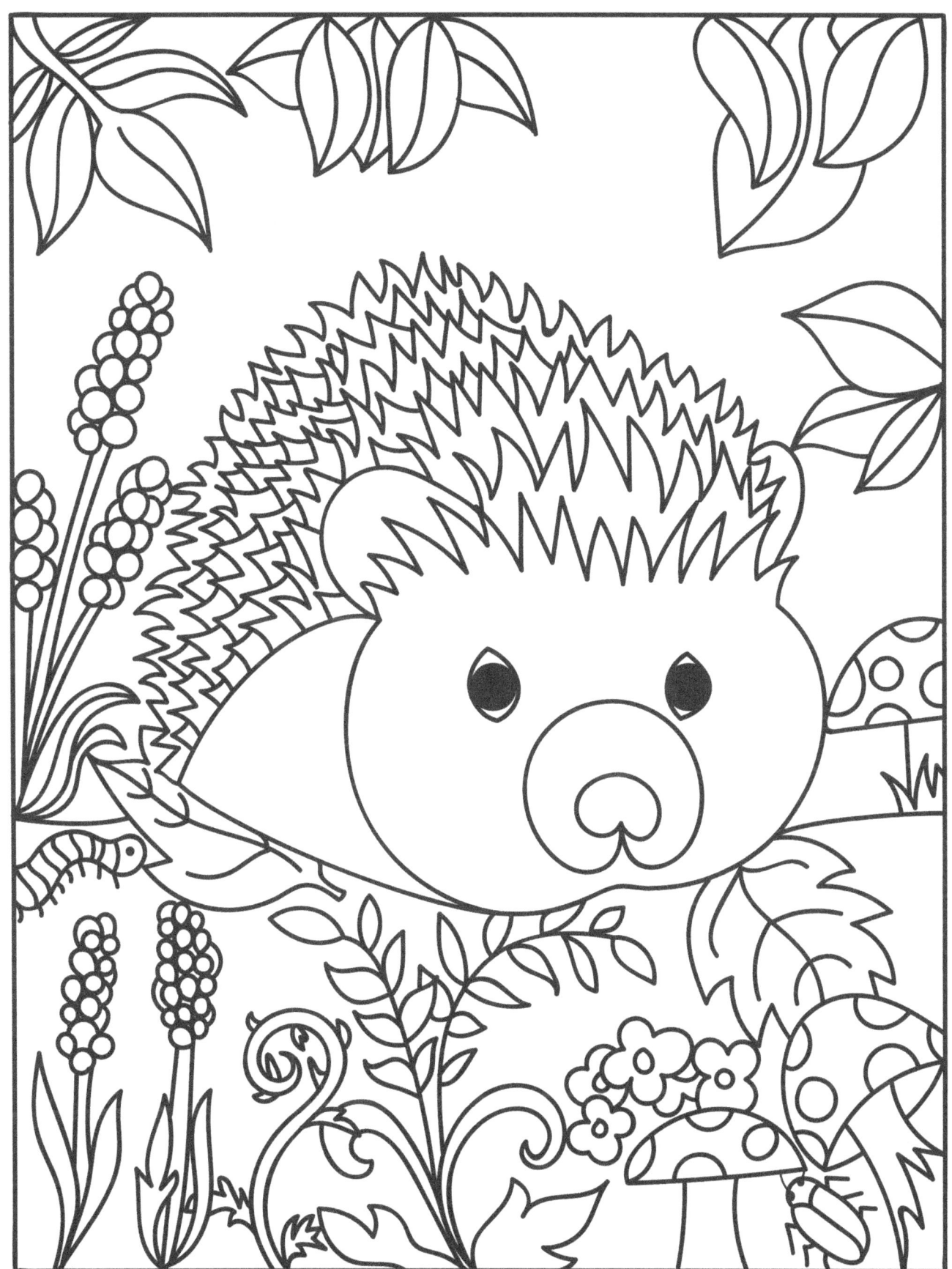

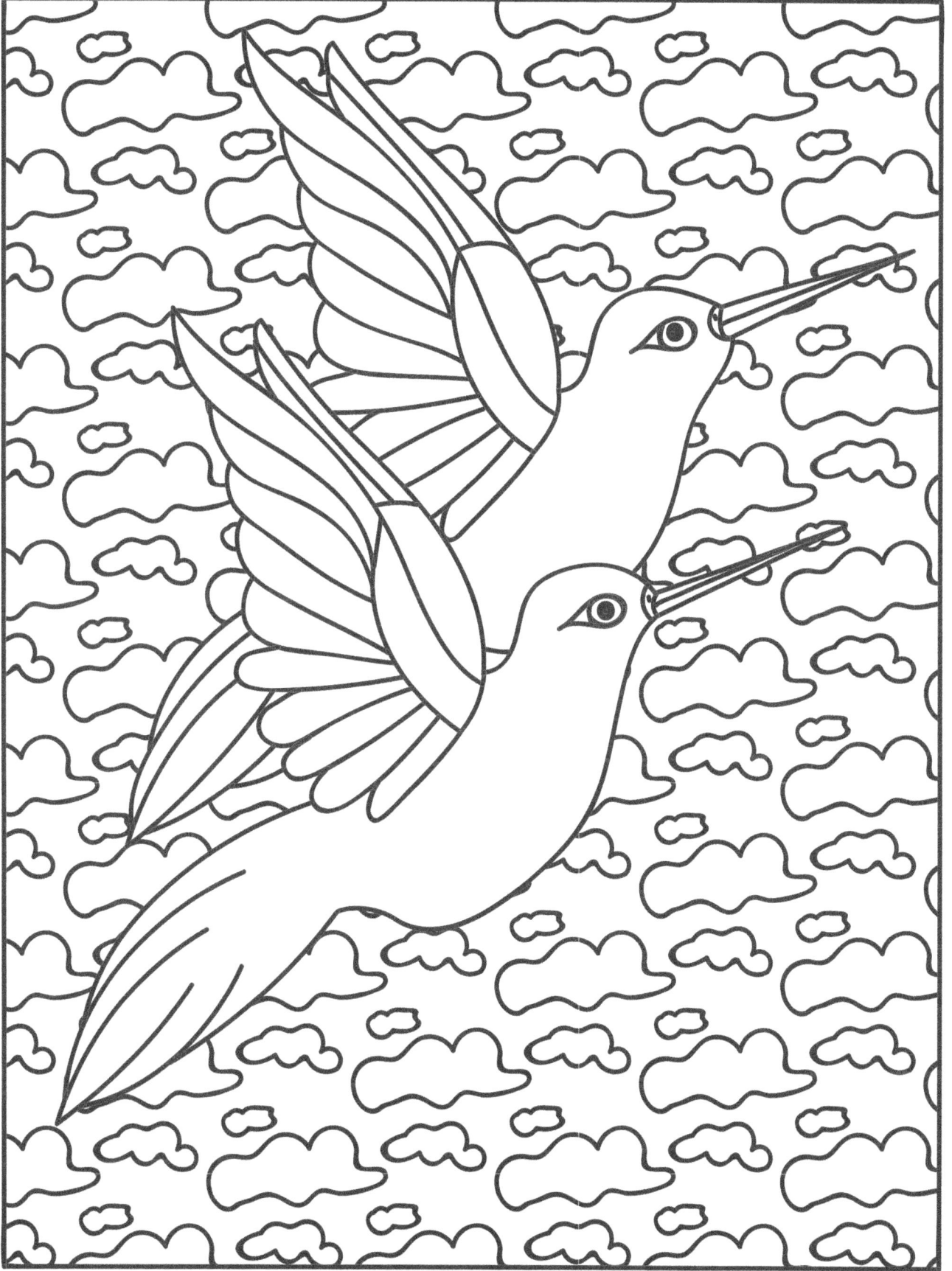

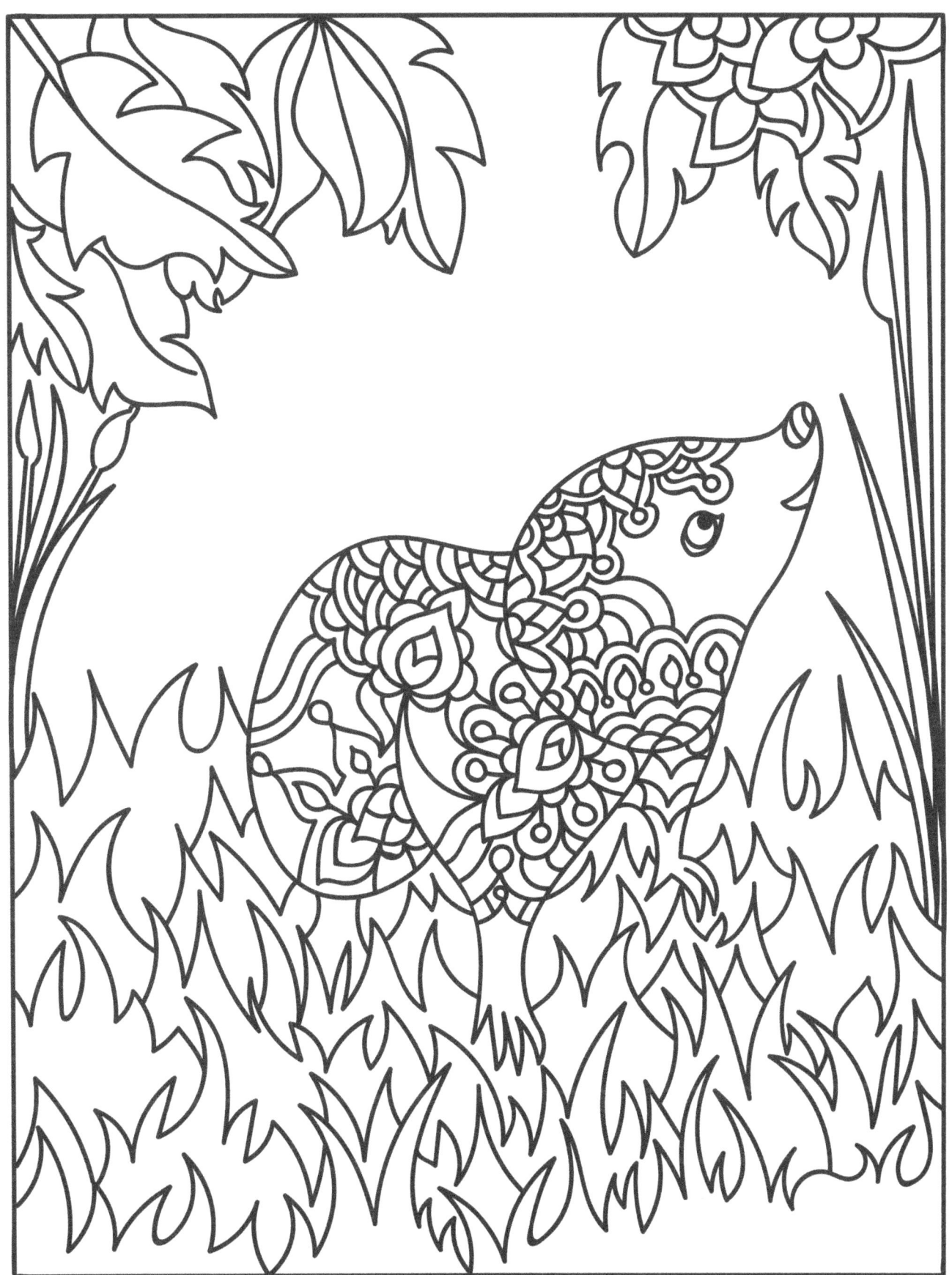

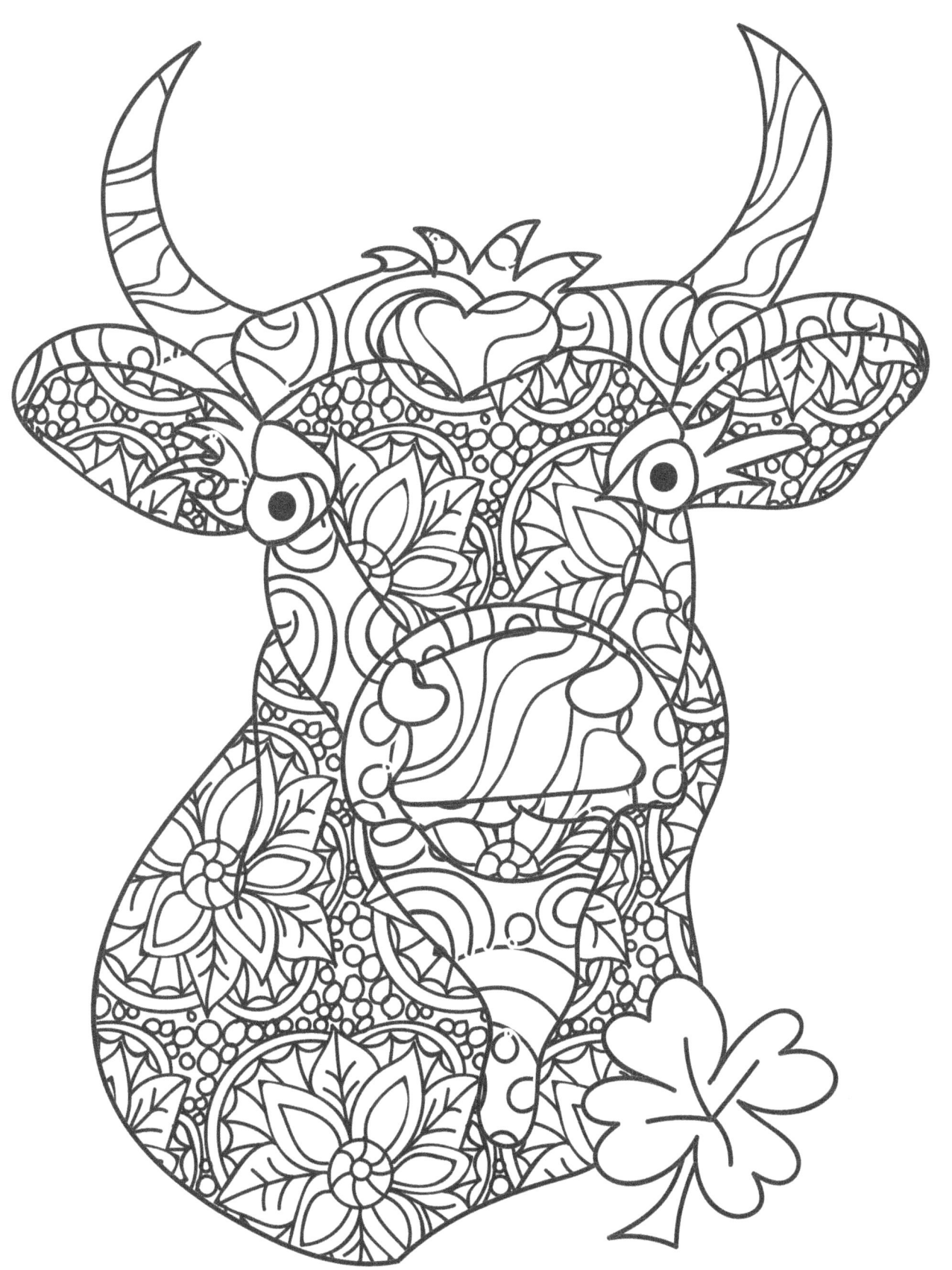

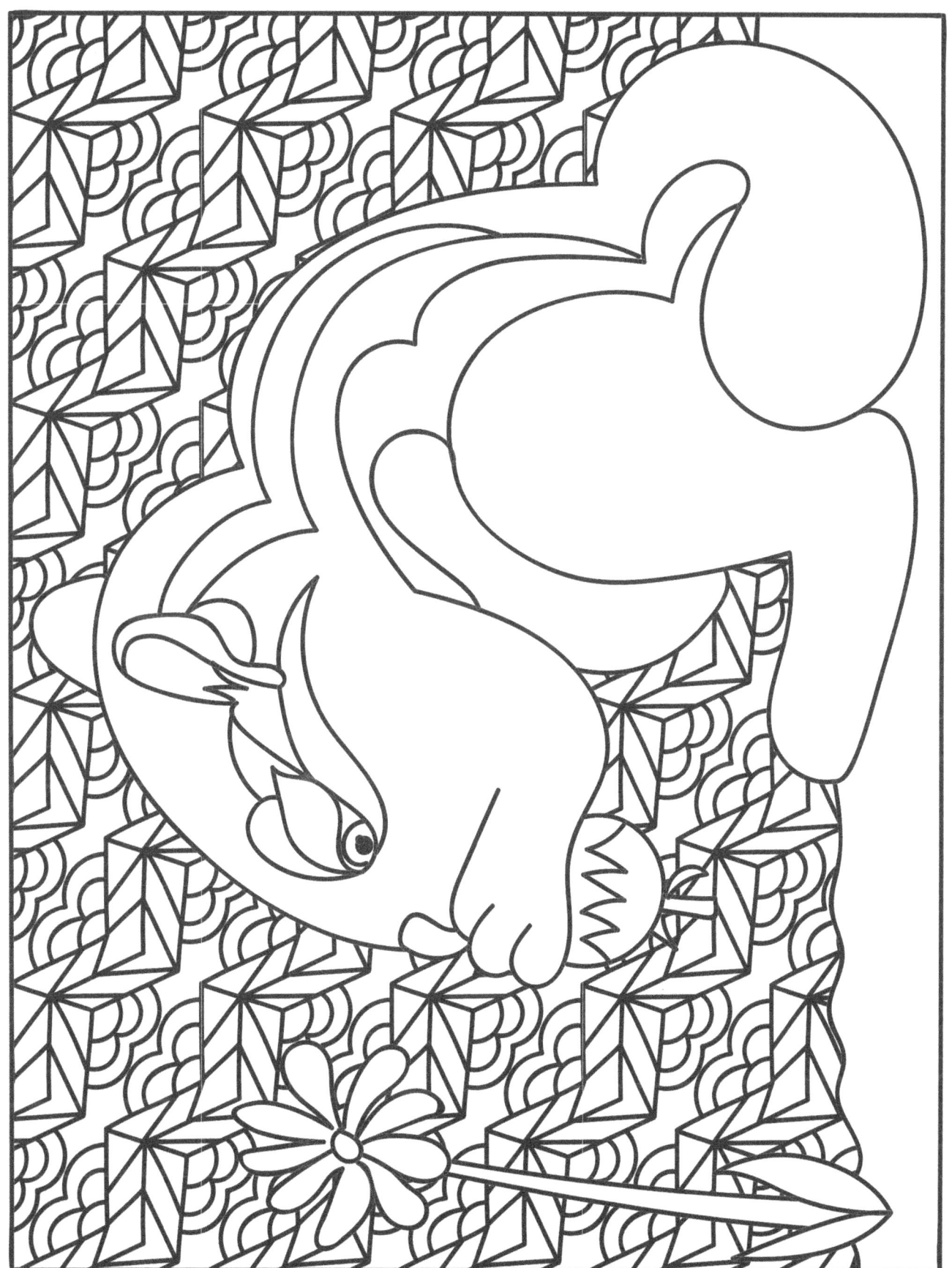

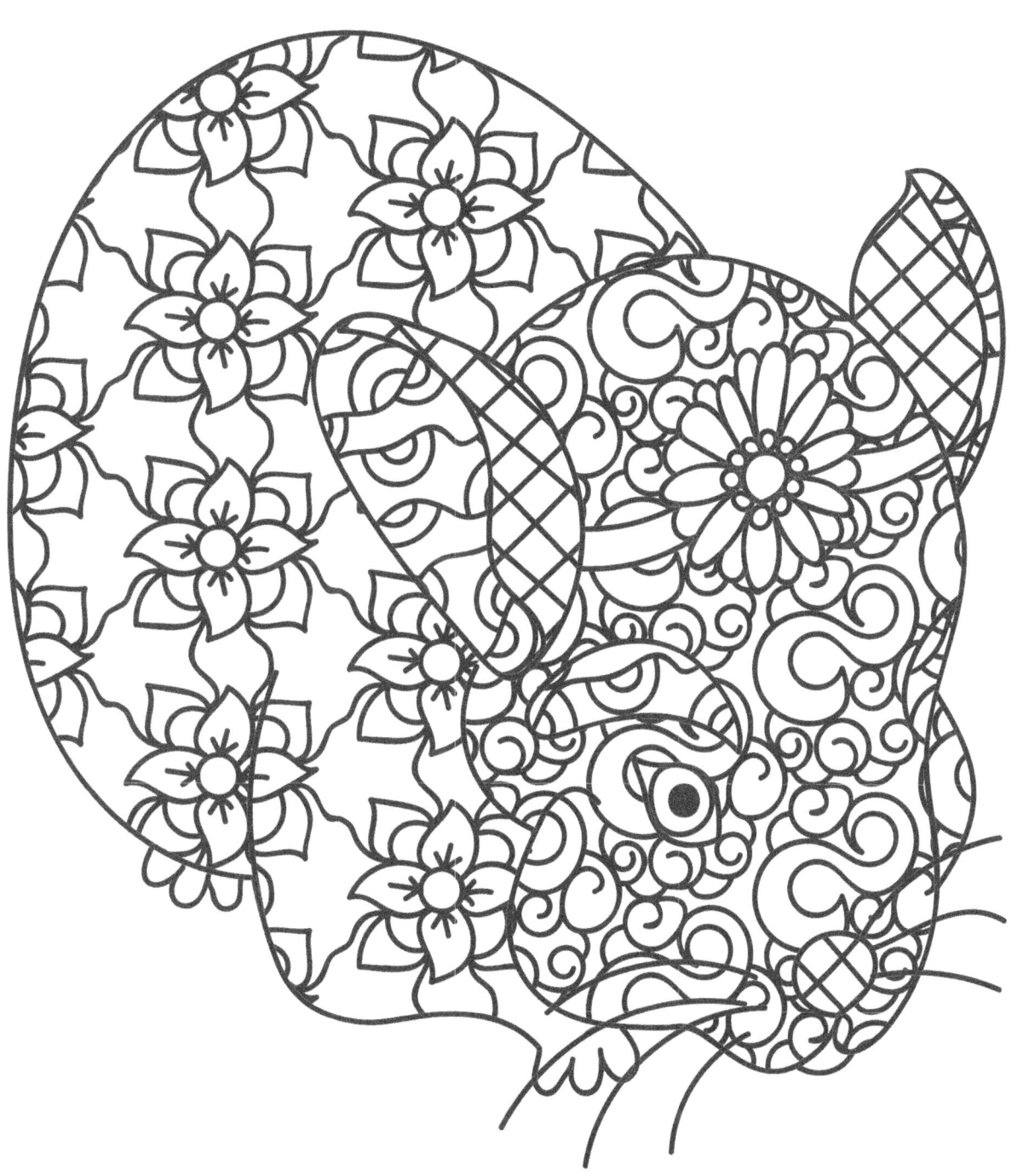

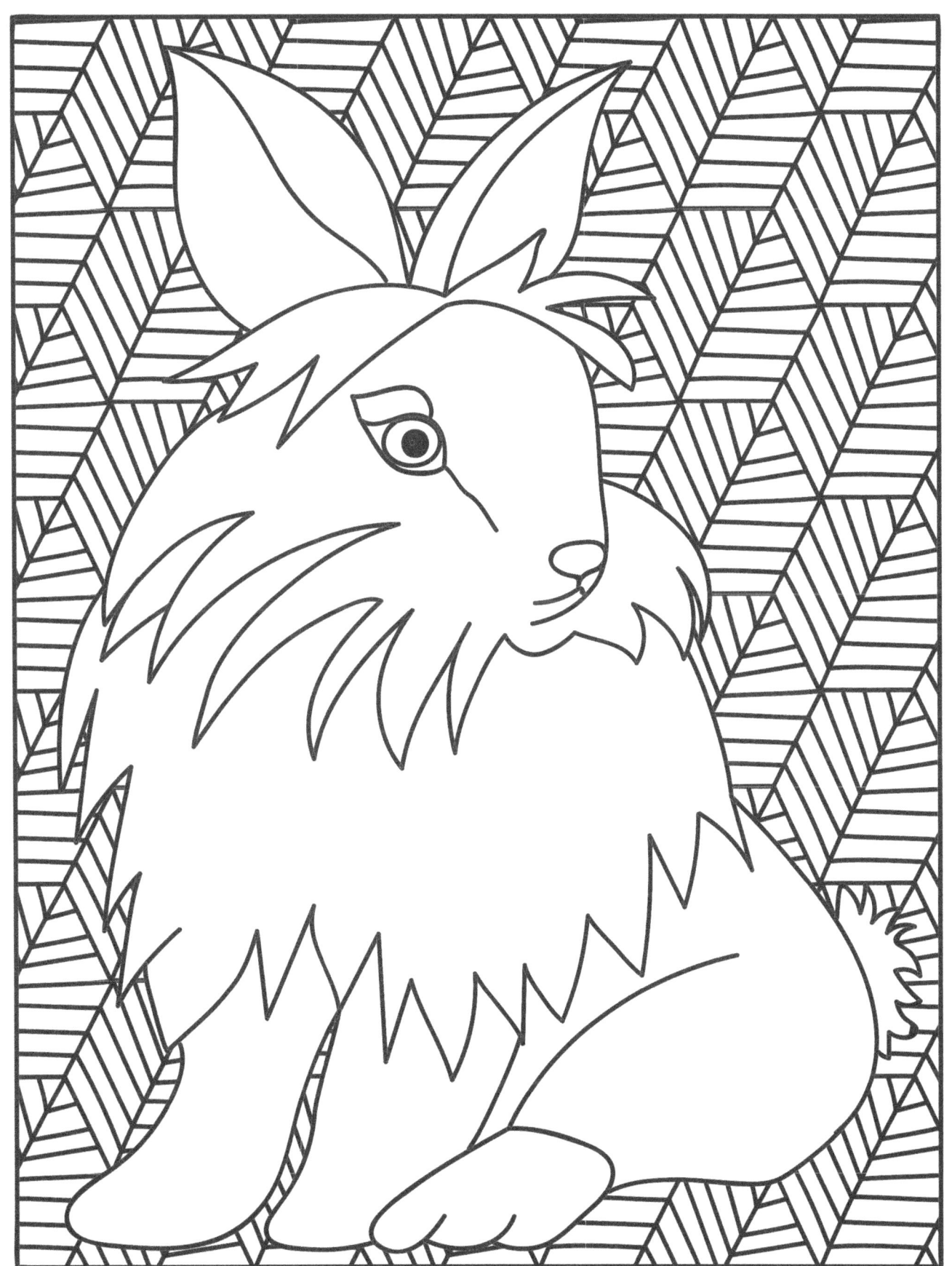

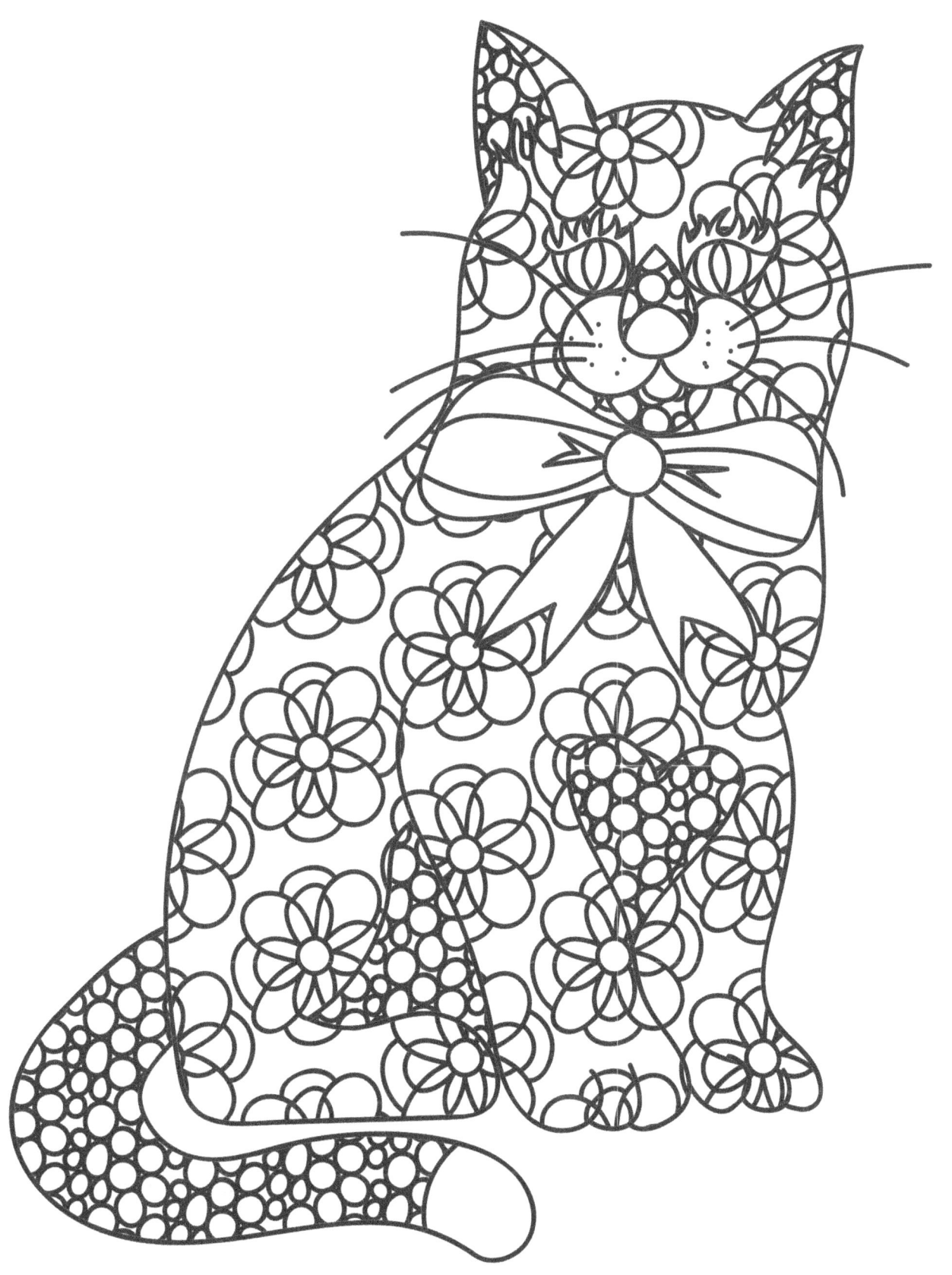

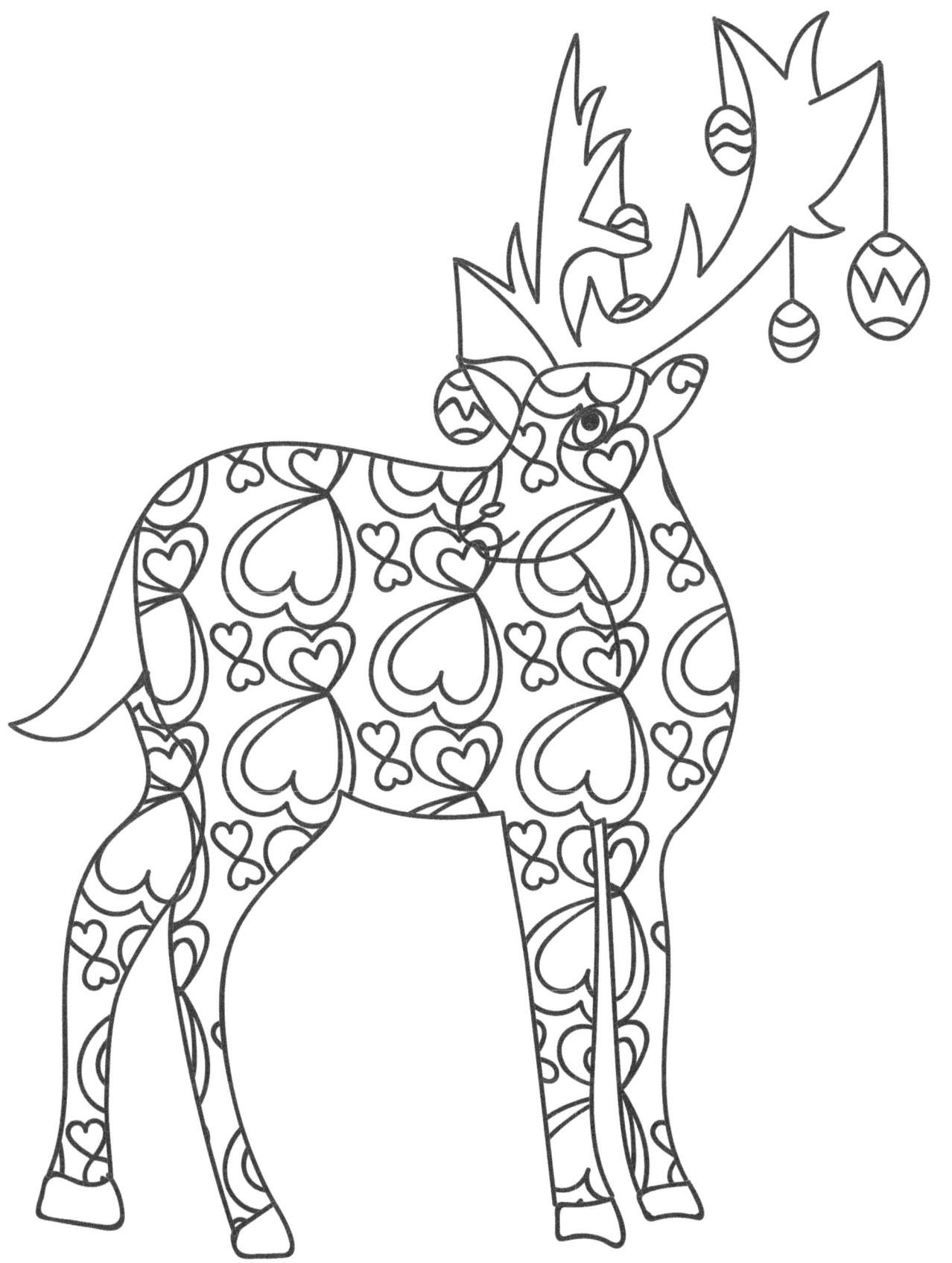

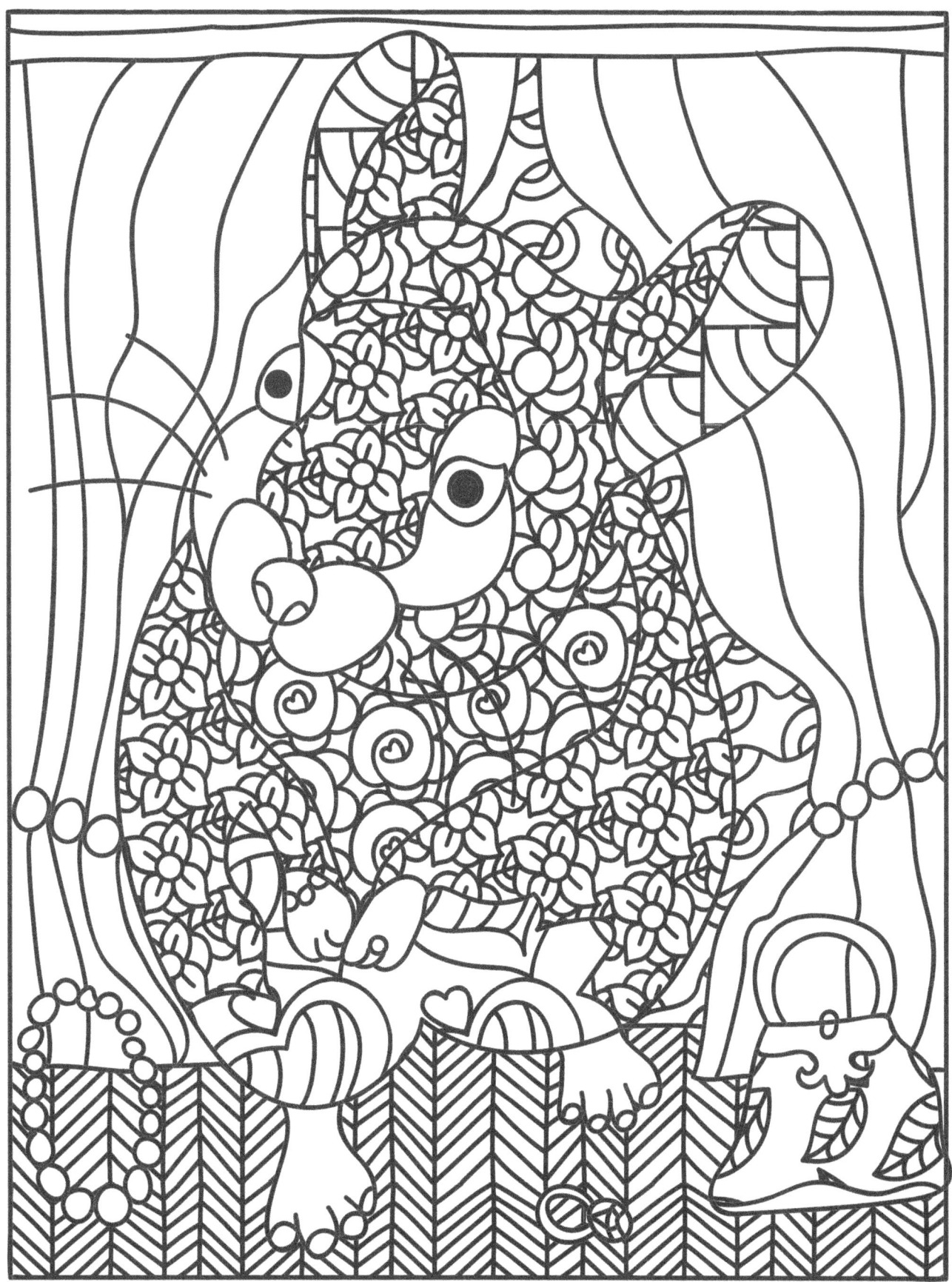

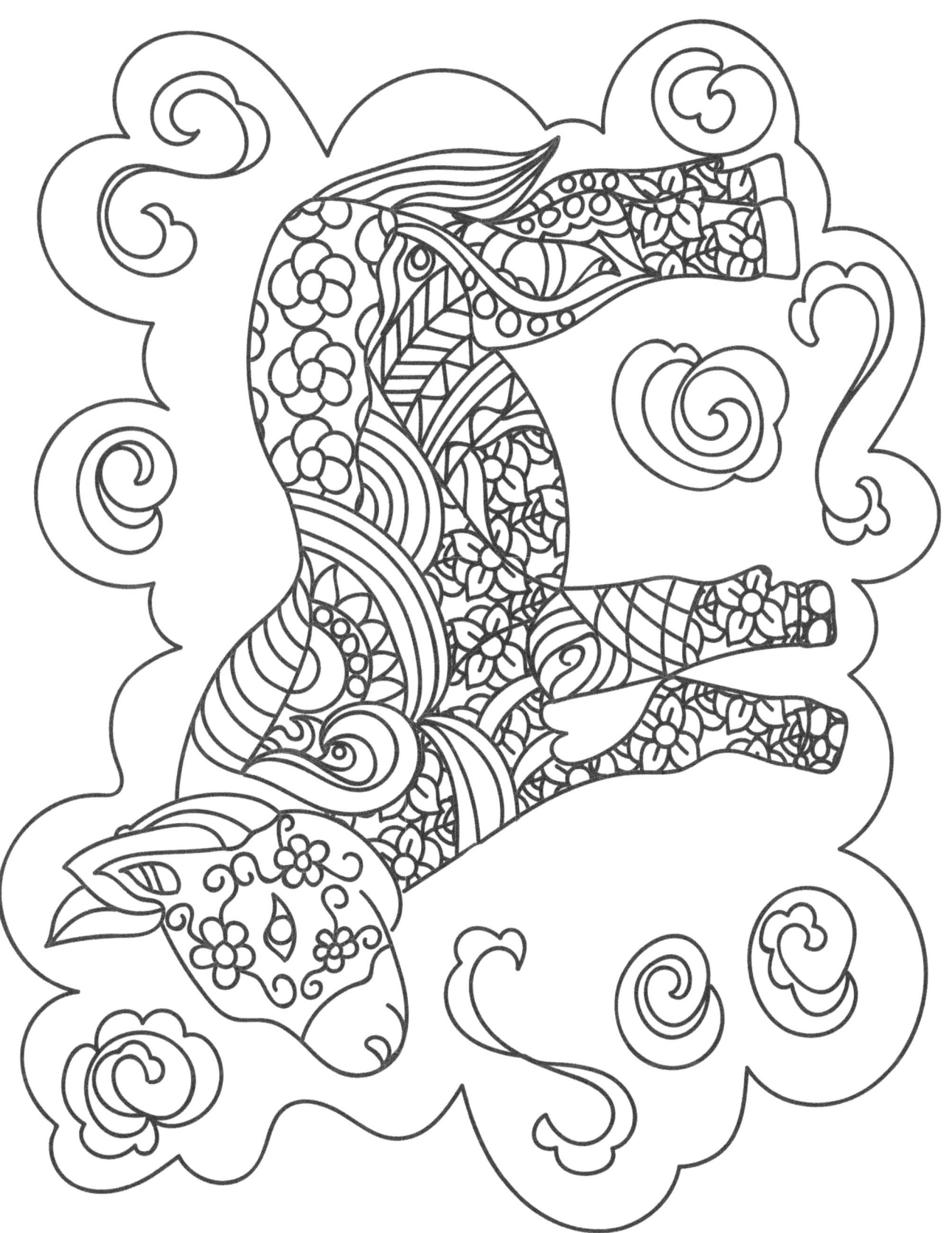

COLOR TEST PAGE

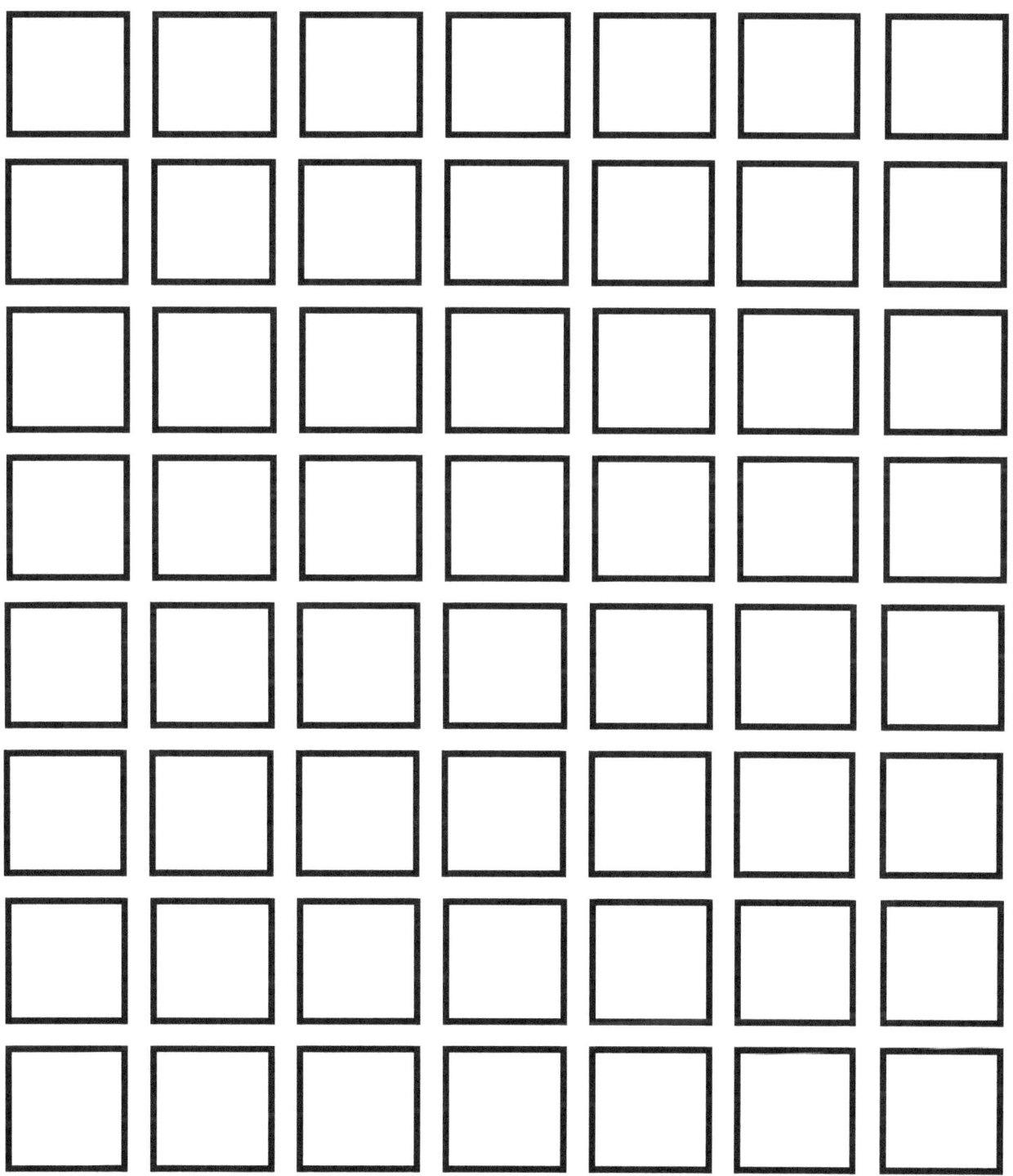

COLOR TEST PAGE

www.ingramcontent.com/pod-product-compliance
Lightning Source LLC
Chambersburg PA
CBHW081616220526
45468CB00010B/2900